ART, POWER, DIPLOMACY

Government Art Collection
The Untold Story

Foreword by Nicholas Serota

Penny Johnson
Julia Toffolo
Richard Dorment
Cornelia Parker
Andrew Renton
Adrian George

Published by
Scala Publishers Ltd
Northburgh House
10 Northburgh Street
London EC1V 0AT
www.scalapublishers.com

In association with Government Art Collection
www.gac.culture.gov.uk

ISBN: 978–1–85759–691–5

Design by: Park Studio
Copy editor: Sarah Kane
Project manager, Scala: Oliver Craske
Printed in Italy

10 9 8 7 6 5 4 3 2 1

Page 1:
fig.1
Unknown
Lady Arabella Stuart (1575–1615)
Cousin of King James VI & I, c.1605
Oil on canvas

CONTENTS

FOREWORD

Nicholas Serota

This book is the first survey of the Government Art Collection (GAC) – a unique British cultural organisation – and is published to coincide with the first exhibition of the Collection held in a public gallery.

Tate has been closely involved with the history and development of the GAC since 1935, when the Office of Works set up a 'Picture Committee' to advise on the acquisition of works of art for government buildings. The members of the committee consisted of the directors of the Tate Gallery, National Gallery and National Portrait Gallery. The first Tate director to sit on the committee was James Bolivar Manson, and seven decades later the close association continues with the *ex officio* position held by Penelope Curtis, director, Tate Britain.

Throughout this time, the committee has given advice on the GAC's acquisitions of works of art and, increasingly, in regards to its role of promoting Britain through the display of works in major government buildings in the UK and overseas.

The GAC is, to all intents and purposes, a museum, acquiring, researching, conserving, interpreting and displaying over 13,500 works of art. Unlike a museum, however, its holdings are not displayed in one place, but instead on the walls of thousands of rooms in hundreds of buildings in nearly every capital city worldwide. It has a unique role in presenting and promoting British art in non-museum environments – government offices, meeting rooms and the public spaces of official residences – to people who might never have made the conscious decision to look at art in a museum. Intriguingly, the art that is selected from the Collection to represent Britain is able to be seen and interpreted in many different ways, giving rise to the many interesting narratives that this publication will reveal for the first time.

Unlike any other public collection, the GAC's presence in the heart of central government and the locations where its holdings are displayed mean that the organisation is directly affected by fast-changing domestic and international events. The present publication articulates this aspect of the GAC's story, showing how works of art have literally formed a backdrop to some of the world's most significant political moments.

The five chapters of this book cover various aspects of the GAC's role in representing British art, culture and history. The Government Art

fig.2
David Roberts
The Great Staircase, Stafford House
[now Lancaster House], 1832
Oil on canvas

Collection remains a truly British institution – many countries have not, for whatever reason, been able to establish similar organisations – and after more than 100 years of existence it seems a good moment to step back and look at its achievements. I am very pleased to welcome a publication celebrating a collection that works behind the scenes to promote the culture of Britain, our art and our artists.

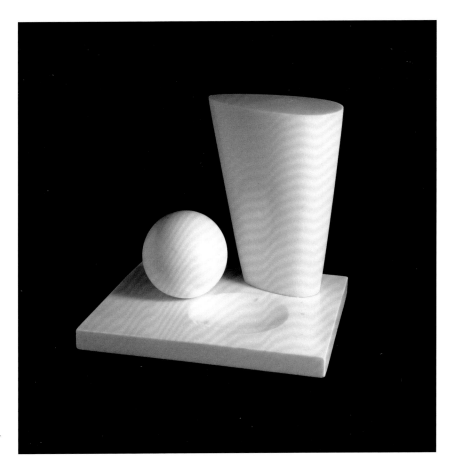

fig.3
Hurvin Anderson
Peter's 1, 2007
Oil on canvas

fig.4
Barbara Hepworth
Conoid, Sphere and Hollow III, 1937
Marble

1. TURNING THE WORLD INSIDE OUT: THE ART OF CHOOSING FOR GOVERNMENT

Penny Johnson

> Godfrey (TV producer): Well it's up to you, obviously, Prime Minister. All I can say is that if that's what you are going to say I suggest a very modern suit, high tech furniture, high energy yellow wallpaper, abstract paintings, in fact everything to disguise the absence of anything new in the actual speech…
>
> Jim Hacker (Prime Minister): I'd like to go back to my original dynamic speech – you know about the grand design.
>
> Godfrey (TV producer): Fine, then it's the reassuring traditional background, dark suit, oak panelling, leather volumes, 18th-century portraits.
>
> *Yes Prime Minister: The Ministerial Broadcast*, BBC TV, Series 1, Episode 2, 1986

I was lucky enough to catch a repeat of this episode of *Yes Minister* not long after I started as director of the Government Art Collection (GAC) in April 1997. In this scene, the Prime Minister Jim Hacker is in a characteristic flap about the messages which might be read into the art displayed behind him during his televised address to the nation. It is not uncommon to see works of art in the background on TV or in newspapers when government ministers are being interviewed or welcoming visiting dignitaries. What is not revealed, however, is that these works of art have been selected for the most part from the GAC and have generally been on the walls for some time, rather than temporarily shipped in to create the right impression as suggested in the scene from *Yes Minister*. The selection of works – especially those chosen by the Prime Minister – is a source of fascination for the people I meet, including visitors to the Collection and the press, probably because we all like to think it may give us a clue as to the personality and taste of the selector. Do the works of art reflect the person who chose them, or are they a mask? I am not able to give a succinct answer to that question, but having worked at the GAC for more than a decade I am able to offer an overview of our role and why art continues to play a part in ministers' lives.

In the course of the last 113 years, the British government has collected over 13,500 works of mostly British art from the 16th century to the present day in a broad range of styles and media. In this idiosyncratic

fig.5
Vanessa Bell
Byzantine Lady, 1912
Oil on board

fig.6
Joseph Wilton
*Oliver Cromwell (1599–1658),
Lord Protector of England,
Scotland and Ireland, c.1762*
Marble

Collection there are about 2,400 oil paintings by artists such as William
Hogarth, Thomas Gainsborough and Vanessa Bell (fig.5), an impressive
range of about 8,400 prints, some 1,700 drawings and watercolours
including works by Edward Lear, Edward Burra and Edward Bawden,
400 photographs by such artists as Fay Godwin, Paul Graham and Isaac
Julien and about 280 sculptures including pieces by Joseph Wilton
(fig.6), Barbara Hepworth and Anish Kapoor's *Turning the World Inside
Out* (fig.7). There are also textiles, videos and mixed media works.
As might be expected in a collection of British art, landscape is
particularly well represented, as are topographical prints, but there
are also intriguing portraits of amongst others Elizabeth I (fig.8), the

1st Duke of Wellington and David Lloyd George, as well as a number of abstract paintings by such artists as Ivon Hitchens, Prunella Clough and Fiona Rae.

There are certainly some surprising omissions, notably the absence of paintings by J. M. W. Turner, Francis Bacon or David Hockney, but in this respect the GAC is comparable to many public collections where gaps inevitably occur due to missed opportunities, lack of funds or subject matter not being considered appropriate in former times. The Collection is not intended to constitute a comprehensive survey of British art, but rather to acquire works of art by a wide range of artists for display in the many and distinctive locations we work in. Maybe the Collection's quirkiness should be regarded as one of its strengths. Clearly the journalist John Litchfield thought so when he referred to it as 'a challenging, unconventional art collection' in his article 'Diplomatic Victory in France for British Contemporary Art' (*The Independent*, October 2007).

fig.7
Anish Kapoor
Turning the World Inside Out, 1995
Stainless steel

Works of art for the Government Art Collection are acquired for a specific purpose – for display in government buildings. The fact that these works are shown in major British government buildings across the UK and in nearly every capital city around the world helps to promote British art while contributing to cultural diplomacy and creating a visual representation of Britain. Our promotional role extends to commissioning art for new or refurbished government buildings in London and abroad (see chapter 5). Since the Collection came into being, the particular needs and requirements of successive governments have inevitably altered the course of its history. The core purpose, however, to promote British art and artists, developed relatively early and has remained. We are part of, and funded by, the Department for Culture, Media and Sport (DCMS) and based in London where works are temporarily housed, either for conservation or in transit between different locations.

The GAC's promotional role dates back to the 1930s, when the Collection was considerably smaller and its global reach was not so extensive. The works are mostly displayed in the offices of ministers, Permanent Secretaries (the Sir Humphreys of this world, to stay with *Yes Minister*) and senior officials, Whitehall entrance halls (fig.9) and meeting rooms, as well as in the public representational areas of embassies and the residences of ambassadors, high commissioners and consuls-general in nearly every capital city of the world. Around two-thirds of the Collection is always on show in about 400 buildings (about one-third in the UK and two-thirds abroad) – the GAC can essentially be seen as the largest, most dispersed public collection of British art in the world, with thousands of people seeing the works in many different spaces and places. If the core role of the Collection is to select art for government buildings so as to promote Britain and its considerable artistic achievements, the works of art also enhance working environments and provide stimulating spaces. The Collection exists to ensure that buildings which represent Britain in the UK or abroad have an appropriate and distinctive appearance, commensurate with Britain's role in the world. As Jack Straw (Foreign Secretary, 2001–06) has pointed out, '… to those who dispute the importance of the GAC, one could ask what our Posts abroad would feel like with bare walls?'[1] Many other ministers have commented on the importance of the Collection, including George Osborne, the current Chancellor of the Exchequer, who remarked, 'In Britain we have some of the best art in the world, and the Government Art Collection does a great job of showcasing what we have to offer.'[2]

We are not the only country to run a government art collection. There are similar organisations, for example, in Australia, Belgium, Canada, France, Germany, the Netherlands, Ireland and the US that curate and

fig.8
Marcus Gheeraerts the Younger
Queen Elizabeth I (1533–1603), Reigned 1558–1603, 1592–1603
Oil on panel

fig.9
Special to You, 1999 by
Daniel Sturgis in entrance Hall,
22 Whitehall, London, 2005

install displays in their government buildings, but not all of them do so with their own collections or have works of art spanning over five centuries. We do, however, share many of the same challenges – such as the geographical spread of works, the exhibiting of art in non-gallery environments, and the need to manage the expectations of recipients – something that we learned when the GAC organised the first meeting of comparable collections in 2003.

As might be expected, we are at our busiest after the election of a new government and during ministerial reshuffles. Works of art can signify the arrival of a new incumbent much more readily than other changes that ministers may wish to introduce. Ministers usually choose their

fig.10
Ed Vaizey, Minister for Culture, selecting work with Penny Johnson, Director of the GAC, May 2010

fig.11
Installation of *Howling Like Dogs, I Swallowed Solid Air*, 1998–2003 by **Zarina Bhimji**, Office of Margaret Hodge, Minister for Culture, November 2009

works by visiting the GAC, where we will have pre-selected a number of works from the Collection (fig.10). This pre-selection is based on our knowledge of the Collection, the architecture and scale of the minister's office and what might be appropriate to reflect their portfolio of work. We then either agree on a final selection or we look at other possibilities; occasionally a minister selects work with comparatively little input from us. The selected works are then prepared for dispatch by the GAC team of specialists; the transport arrangements are made by the registrar and we supervise the installation to ensure that the art is hung to its best advantage (fig.11). Interpretative material is also provided for locations, so that all recipients are knowledgeable about the works of art and can pass this information on to their visitors.

However, as David Lammy (Minister for Culture, 2005–07) suggested, selecting works is more complex than merely covering a wall:

> Many, many people come into my office, people from all over the world, people from all across our arts sector, and what they are seeing in my office is not my art. It is a showcase of British art. In the 21st century, in a world dominated by India, China, the United States and by a reformed Europe, one of the edges that we in Britain have is our creativity and our culture. The GAC is an opportunity to showcase that art because the world's opinion formers every day of the week come into ministerial offices, come into our embassies, and we are making a really bold statement about what we can do.[3]

fig.12
Office of David Lammy, Minister for Culture 2005–07, November 2005

Here Lammy's comment about showcasing British art highlights the GAC's promotional role, but it also underlines the importance of selecting the right kind of works of art to display (fig.12). While works are chosen because they are, in themselves, strong works, they are also often chosen because they have specific connections to a location or even a particular person's role. Notable examples of specific connections between works of art and Whitehall departments include the painting *The Judge and his Clerk* (1949) by Merlyn Evans, which has been hung in the office of the Secretary of State in the Ministry of Justice; the wonderfully evocative *Aldgate East 1* by Jock McFadyen in the office of the Secretary of State for Transport (fig.13); and the portrait of the ambassador Sir Henry Wotton, who famously declared that 'an ambassador is an honest man sent abroad to lie for the good of his country', which has been on the walls of the Permanent Secretary of the Foreign and Commonwealth Office for many years. Not surprisingly, the intriguing pair of paintings *Resuscitation by Dr. Hawes of Man Believed Drowned* (fig.14) and *Young Man Lifted from a River, Apparently Drowned* by Robert Smirke (1752–1845) were for several years exhibited in a conference room of the Department of Health and are now back there, in a minister's office. Sometimes, a minister's constituency is represented with an historical topographical print – for example by Samuel and Nathaniel Buck. Another painting with a strong relevance to its location is Thomas Ross's portrait of Oliver Cromwell's spymaster John Thurloe, which is displayed in the office

fig.13
Jock McFadyen
Aldgate East, 1997
Oil on canvas

fig.14
Robert Smirke
*Resuscitation by Dr. Hawes of Man
Believed Drowned, c.1787*
Oil on canvas

of the Chief of the Secret Intelligence Service at Vauxhall Cross
overlooking the Thames (fig.15).

Some works can accrue multiple meanings depending on the context.
For example, Paul Boateng, Chief Secretary to the Treasury between
2002 and 2005, chose *Peas are the New Beans* by Bob and Roberta
Smith (see fig.50) for his waiting room and recalled this with humour
in 2007:

> The most useful piece of art I ever chose… threw a less than
> respectful eye, on that much maligned breed 'bean counters'.
> Cast in the role of 'bean counter in chief', I welcomed
> anything that raised a laugh or at least a wry smile on the
> part of those awaiting scrutiny before they were ushered in
> to my rooms at number 1 Horseguards. The Government Art
> Collection is a valuable national asset. Not only does it survive

Sec.y Thurloe.

fig.16
Grayson Perry with *Print for a Politician*, February 2010

any cost benefit analysis in this particular instance by breaking the ice in the course of any number of spending reviews, it actively promoted efficiency and value for money.[4]

Then in 2005 Sir Gus O'Donnell became the new Cabinet Secretary and spoke of his keenness for civil servants to deliver their work with 'Pace, Passion, Pride and Professionalism' – the four 'Ps'. This led to the playful and richly layered Bob and Roberta Smith painting being reselected for his Whitehall waiting room, where it remained for several years.

Some works seem entirely appropriate for the Collection. Grayson Perry's *Print for a Politician* is a case in point (fig.16). Since its acquisition in 2006, the etching with its very relevant title has been in constant demand for the offices of politicians: it went to the Secretary of State and two Ministers for Culture in the Department for Culture, Media and Sport and, in 2010, to the Chancellor of the Exchequer.

fig.15
Thomas Ross
John Thurloe (1616–1668), Secretary to Oliver Cromwell and Secretary of State
Oil on canvas

For 10 Downing Street, the most prestigious government building, our strategy is to present extensive displays of the Collection that can actively promote British art through the ages to the thousands of people who visit from all over the world. The works range from the 16th century to the present day to reflect the scope of the Collection and include, as might be expected, some of the more important of the GAC's works of art, notably a portrait of Dr James Hamilton by Henry Raeburn (fig.17), a

21

fig.18
Jean Baptiste van Loo (Studio)
*Robert Walpole, 1st Earl of Orford
(1676–1745), Prime Minister, c.1740*
Oil on canvas

fig.17
Sir Henry Raeburn
*Dr James Hamilton Senior (1749–
1835), Edinburgh Physician, c.1790*
Oil on canvas

portrait of Jane Inglis by John Constable (fig.42) and *View of the Thames
from Richmond Hill* by Peter Tillemans (fig.47). We also show works that
demonstrate links with the building and its history: there are portraits
of Robert Walpole, the first Prime Minister (fig.18), and the innovative
designer William Kent, whom Walpole engaged to remodel 10 Downing
Street, which had been given to him as an official residence by King
George II. A fine full-length portrait of the king hangs in the elegant
early 19th-century State Dining Room designed by Sir John Soane.

Modern art at Number 10 is represented with an early landscape by
Lucian Freud (fig.19) and nautical scenes by Paul Nash and Edward
Wadsworth, which are hung adjacent to an area dedicated to regular

fig.19
Lucian Freud
Welsh Landscape, 1939–40
Oil on canvas

selections of more contemporary art. These displays have in recent years included paintings by Michael Craig-Martin, Gillian Carnegie and Gary Hume, photographs by Isaac Julien, Anne Hardy and Runa Islam (fig.20) and videos by Wood and Harrison. Displays in the building are periodically changed when works are lent to public exhibitions or are transferred elsewhere.

Who selects works of art for 10 Downing Street? Not surprisingly, the Prime Minister of the day is preoccupied with other more pressing matters, so we make proposals to a group of Number 10 staff, an arrangement which was established in the late 1990s. It was Cherie Blair who suggested there should be more portraits of women achievers in the State Reception Rooms, as she initially felt there was a predominance of depictions of male sitters. This chimed with our own views and allowed us the opportunity to bring in Margaret Carpenter's wonderful full-length portrait of Ada Lovelace, the mathematician (and daughter of Lord Byron), who worked with Charles Babbage on the calculating engine (fig.21).

In addition to placing works from the Collection, in 2000 we initiated a rolling annual programme that showcases 20th-century British art lent to 10 Downing Street from public galleries and museums outside London. These are placed in the main corridor leading to the Cabinet Room, a prominent thoroughfare where all official visitors walk.

With the election of the Labour government in May 1997, a significant shift occurred in the work of the GAC as the new government saw the potential of contemporary art to promote the idea of a progressive and creative Britain. Providing such a wholesale change of displays would not have been possible without the gifted and committed professional team that I inherited from my predecessor, the inestimable Dr Wendy Baron. The GAC played a key role in suggesting the presentation of a group of works in 10 Downing Street by artists of Tony Blair's generation. Installed within a few months of Blair's election, they included works on paper by Anish Kapoor, Sean Scully, Mark Francis and Thérèse Oulton, all lent by the Tate at a time when the GAC was only beginning to

fig.20
Runa Islam
First Day of Spring (production still),
2005
C-type digital photograph

fig.22
Negotiation by **Michael Craig-Martin**, a temporary display for the European Union Heads of Government Conference, Lancaster House, March 1998

acquire works by such artists. This display helped contribute to the notion of 'Cool Britannia' (as the media called it) – the focus on new trends in contemporary culture that came to be associated with the early days of New Labour.

In November 1997, another predominantly contemporary display of GAC works was installed in the temporary interiors created by Sir Terence Conran for the Anglo-French summit held in Canary Wharf. The location was chosen by the Government for its modernity, in stark contrast to the historic Lancaster House, where such diplomatic events would ordinarily have been held, and the art reinforced the desire for a contemporary, international image. There have been other occasions when the GAC has been approached to provide art for display, for example at Lancaster House for the European Union Heads of Government Conference in 1998 (fig.22) and most recently at the G20 summit at ExCeL, London, in 2009.

Fast forward to May 2010 and the election of the new Coalition government – a busy period in which we worked with some 50 ministers over three months to make selections from the Collection. People are always intrigued to know which works are on ministers' walls and in broad terms about 50 per cent of the ministers decided on modern/contemporary art, 25 per cent historical, and 25 per cent on a mix of both. Jeremy Hunt, the new Secretary of State at DCMS, wanted predominantly contemporary works for his office (fig.23):

fig.21
Margaret Carpenter
Ada, Countess of Lovelace (1815–1852) Mathematician; Daughter of Lord Byron, 1836
Oil on canvas

> As Secretary of State for Culture, my choice of art is one of the most scrutinised in government. Every day I share with my visitors the best of contemporary British art. Whether Yinka Shonibare's *Nelson's Ship in a Bottle* (the smaller

fig.23
Nelson's Ship in a Bottle by
Yinka Shonibare with *Brown's (Mrs E. W. Brown)* and *Brown's (Mr P. J. Brown)* by **Mark Wallinger** in the office of Jeremy Hunt, July 2010

version), or works by Grayson Perry, Sonia Boyce, Mark Wallinger or Tacita Dean, I am proud of the extraordinary talent our country has to offer – and thrilled to have it around me every day.[5]

This demonstrates the degree to which times have changed. Even in the 1990s there was relatively little recently made art in diplomatic buildings, although the Foreign and Commonwealth Office did work with contemporary artists – with some GAC involvement – when commissioning works for new buildings, one example being the British embassy in Dublin (1996). It was in this context that my first visit to a British embassy became so significant. In June 1997 I went to Paris to see the GAC's displays at the ambassador's residence and to meet Sir Michael Jay, the ambassador, who asked me whether the GAC could provide a 'more modern feel' in the residence. This presented a challenge for us because of the elaborate 18th-century interior, arguably the finest of the UK's diplomatic residences. The building also features a number of GAC works that have historical associations with it. By early October that year, in time for British Design week, a group of works specifically acquired for this location, some demonstrating connections with France, were installed in the Glazed Galleries, a 19th-century extension onto the garden. This transformed the space which had previously been lined with full-length replica portraits of monarchs (figs 24 and 25). The new display demonstrated how the Collection contributed to Britain's changing image abroad and encouraged other diplomatic posts to follow suit. We now refresh the contemporary work in Paris every four to five years with each incoming ambassador: to date we've curated three displays.

Incoming ambassadors, high commissioners and consuls-general do not necessarily trigger a fresh display, however. 'Do you change the works with the arrival of a new ambassador in each location?' is one of the questions we are frequently asked by people on our guided tours as well as by new ambassadors. In fact, this is when we have especially to employ our own diplomatic skills to manage such expectations. The distance and spread of the locations means that physically and financially it is just not feasible to make changes every time, but in most cases displays are working well and there is no real need for a change. However, we have a strategy of reviewing and refreshing selections based on a number of factors according to the importance of the location and duration of existing displays. When a new one is initiated, we operate in the same way as with ministers, pre-selecting works and arriving at the final group with the ambassador.

A number of diplomats have provided evidence of how the GAC contributes to cultural diplomacy by enhancing the appearance of locations and encouraging international relationships. Another equally important point is that displays of art can also do much to challenge possible preconceptions about the legacy of Britain's imperial past. As Malcolm Rifkind (Foreign Secretary 1995–97) has put it: '…the art chosen, especially modern art, can help remind visitors that the UK is a modern, vibrant society and not just a repository of imperial mementoes!'[6]

For locations abroad, as within the UK, our modus operandi is to find wherever possible works of art that reflect connections between the artist or subject and the host country, which illuminate shared historical relations and cultural interests. This is perfectly illustrated in the residence in Athens, where Thomas Phillips's magnificent portrait of Lord Byron has been on show since 1953, just after its acquisition

fig.24
Portraits of Queen Victoria
and monarchs, Glazed Gallery,
Ambassador's Residence,
Paris, 1997

fig.25
Contemporary art in the Glazed
Gallery, Ambassador's Residence,
Paris, July 2007

(see fig.84). Lord Byron's participation in the Greek War of Independence made him a national hero in Greece. The removal of his portrait, usually for loan to public exhibitions, however temporary, always causes local concern, as revealed in correspondence to the GAC from the ambassador Sir David Madden:

> Another recent visitor reminded me of the singular esteem in which Lord Byron is held here. Greek first names are either those of saints or ancient philosophers... Against this background a surprising number of Greeks have Byron as a first name with approval from the Church. This is a telling exception, bearing witness to his fame and importance here.[7]

On the other side of the world, in the ambassador's residence in Beijing, a fascinating group of works tells the story of the first British diplomatic mission to China between 1792 and 1794. There is a portrait in pastel of Lord George Macartney, the British envoy; a number of prints recording the trip, which are taken from the original drawings by William Alexander, the artist who accompanied the envoy (fig.26); and a mid-19th-century portrait of Sir George Thomas Staunton, who as a young boy travelled on the voyage to China with his father, the envoy's secretary. Twentieth-century works include circus scenes by Laura Knight and Cosmo Clark (fig.119) and the unusual *The Ministers, Ming Tombs*,

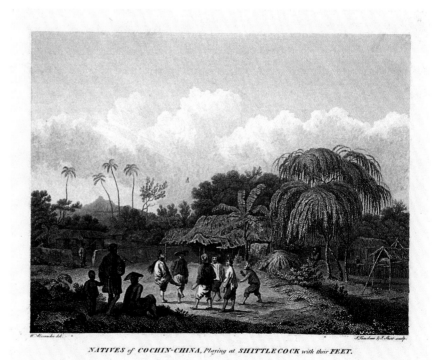

NATIVES of COCHIN-CHINA, Playing at SHITTLE COCK with their FEET.

London, Published April 11 1796 by G. Nicol.

fig.26
William Alexander
Natives of Cochin-China, playing at Shittlecock with their Feet, 1796
Engraving

fig.27
Hannah Starkey
March 2002
C-type photograph

Peking by Stanley Spencer (see fig.113), one of two paintings to come out of a visit he made as part of a British Council tour to China in 1954. Amongst the contemporary work is Hannah Starkey's *March 2002* (fig.27) an enigmatic photograph of a woman in a Chinese restaurant in London and, in the adjacent embassy building, *The Great Bear* by Simon Patterson, a reworking of the iconic London Underground map with one line devoted to Chinese personalities, including politicians and actors.

The value of placing works that have cultural links to a specific location is demonstrated by the feedback we have received from diplomatic representatives in New York. There are displays in each of the three residences in the city – those of the British consul-general and the Permanent and Deputy Permanent Representatives to the United Nations. The art can play a specific role, as Sir John Sawers, the former ambassador to the United Nations, explains: 'Modern British art sets the stage for modern British diplomacy. The art demonstrates style, quality and a distinctive British approach, as we try to do in our diplomacy too. It also generates enthusiasm and helps people relax.'[8]

Sir Alan Collins, the current consul-general in New York City, has commented on the positive effect that an art display can have on guests at his regular diplomatic receptions, explaining how the works can act as 'an icebreaker, a talking point and a great means of showing that the creative arts are a real British strength – that we make this effort to showcase British art has a real impact on our representational work'.[9]

Sir Alan is helped in his role to promote trade by a particularly relevant group of works spanning the 17th century to the present: a portrait of

fig.29
Patrick Heron
*Horizontal Painting with Soft
Black Squares*, 1959
Oil on canvas

fig.28
John Michael Wright
*King James II and VII (1633–1701),
Reigned 1685–8, when Duke of York*
Oil on canvas

fig.30
Rachel Whiteread
Water Tower Project, 1998
Screenprint with acrylic varnish

King James II, after whom, as Duke of York, the city was named when the English captured the colony of New Amsterdam in 1664 (fig.28); *Horizontal Painting with Soft Black Squares* by Patrick Heron, which reveals the influence of American Abstract Expressionism (fig.29), and *Water Tower Project* by Rachel Whiteread (fig.30). This is a print she made in connection with the Public Art Fund Project in New York for which she produced a life-size translucent resin cast of the interior of a wooden water tank of the type so prevalent on the city's skyline.

The value placed on the presentation of works from the Collection was also demonstrated when Sir Mark Lyall-Grant, the current UK Permanent Representative to the UN in New York, wrote about the art in his residence:

> The works of art are important in setting an appropriate and stimulating environment for official visitors to the residence. Ideally, they should combine elements of UK culture, the UK/US link and UN themes. Some of the current artwork does that… Comments from guests include the remark that the art reflects a young and modern image, fresh and challenging.[10]

In Cairo, alongside 19th-century atmospheric and exotic views of Egypt by such artists as David Roberts and Edward Lear and the colourful portrait by Jean Borely of Charles Irby (fig.31), a British naval officer and traveller depicted in oriental dress, there are a number of contemporary works. These include the evocative turquoise painting *Mud on the Nile* by Howard Hodgkin and a sculpture, *Tribute to Sir John Soane*, made of the strikingly beautiful red Egyptian imperial porphyry stone by Stephen Cox. With its array of coloured lines in red, blue, turquoise and yellow with black and white, *Reflection* by Bridget Riley might seem like a painting with a less obvious reason to be in Cairo (see fig.60). However, the colours in this abstract work are inspired by the palette used by ancient Egyptian artists in their wall paintings in the tombs of Upper Egypt. This is a good example of where the association is more subtle, but it nonetheless underlines the interest of contemporary British artists in Egyptian culture.

There is, of course, no one way in which displays of works of art from the Collection contribute to cultural diplomacy. People will always have different interests and tastes, and some will gravitate more towards the historic than contemporary works, and vice versa. In this regard it was interesting to receive the following comment from Sir Peter Westmacott, the ambassador in Paris:

> I have no doubt that the works of art which hang on the walls of the residence make a significant contribution to its impact. The paintings of the Duke of Wellington and Pauline Borghese

fig.31
Jean Baptiste Borely
Charles Leonard Irby (1789–1845), Naval officer and traveller, 1819
Oil on canvas

fig.33
The artist **Cornelia Parker** with her work *Rorscharch (Endless Column III)*, 2006, silver-plated objects, wire and metal

(fig.32) attract most comment for obvious reasons [the Duke of Wellington bought the building from Pauline Borghese, Napoleon's sister, in 1814]… Amongst the contemporary art, the new Cornelia Parker work [*Rorscharch (Endless Column III)*] (fig.33) is going down very well. People from all walks of life find it 'magical'.[11]

fig.32
Portraits of the Duke of Wellington and Pauline Borghese, Ambassador's Residence, Paris

fig.34
Wanjiru Hinga, Residence Manager in front of *E34RR* portfolio of prints, High Commissioner's Residence, Nairobi, December 2010

Another equally fascinating observation was made by Wanjiru Hinga, the residence manager at the high commissioner's residence in Kenya, about the display there (fig.34):

> It brings out, for example, the non-political angle of the UK relations in Kenya and exposes certain social challenges in the UK through the paintings, therefore sharing some insights for visitors who have not been to the UK and have not had the chance to experience the culture there.[12]

This idea, that cultural value might depend entirely on where and by whom it is viewed, was echoed in a remark by Robert Chatterton Dickson and Teresa Albor, the former ambassador to Skopje and his

wife, who recalled: '…we wanted to present the UK as a modern, diverse contemporary society and culture…'[13] Other diplomats find it is the historical association that works of art can underline that help them in their diplomatic work. For example, Boyd McCleary, the former high commissioner in Kuala Lumpur (2006–10) relates how he benefited from:

> … a number of works… which related to Britain's involvement in Malaya/Malaysia; the two fine copper engravings of Prince of Wales Island (now Penang) remind visitors of the length of our engagement in the country and the strong cultural and architectural heritage we left behind.[14]

Similarly, Jenoliya David, a member of staff at the high commission in Colombo, Sri Lanka, believes that 'Having works of art that belong to a century ago drawn by British artists (about Ceylon) shows the long tie between the two countries and the attraction our country has on the British'.[15]

This theme of art bringing two nations together is endorsed by Sir Michael Arthur, high commissioner in New Delhi from 2003 to 2007, whose comment indicates how the GAC can help to represent a change in relations between two countries:

> With your help we hung an Anish Kapoor… I regularly made the point to the thousands of visitors coming through the room that this was to demonstrate the huge distance Britain and India had come together and that at the start of the 21st century one of our and the world's best artists is a UK resident/ national of Bombay birth.[16]

Sometimes, historical events enable works to be shown in locations that were previously politically off limits. A good example of this would be Derek Boshier's challenging painting *I Wonder What My Heroes Think of the Space Race*, installed in the ambassador's residence in Moscow in 2010 (fig.35). As this work refers to the ideological battle for space technology and exploration that dominated American and Soviet politics during the Cold War, the exhibiting of this work in this location would previously have been considered too provocative.

The colourful and exotic painting *The Valley of Mexico* by Daniel Egerton was given by Lord Wakefield to the Collection in 1936 with the express desire that it be displayed at the ambassador's residence in Mexico City (fig.36). The placing of it in Mexico helped to shape the policy of making connections between art and the location that continues seven decades on. In the words of the current ambassador,

fig.35
Derek Boshier
I Wonder What My Heroes Think of the Space Race, 1962
Oil on canvas

fig.36
Daniel Thomas Egerton
The Valley of Mexico, 1837
Oil on canvas

Judith MacGregor, 'His painting is invariably a subject of conversation and interest (not least in this year of Mexico's bicentenary celebrations) but also commands respect as one of the more valuable works of art produced by British artists who have lived and worked in this country.'[17]

It is clear from all the comments we have received from current and former diplomats over the years that displays of art – wherever they are placed in the world – often create a stir and always get people talking. If works of art can be considered as the starting point for conversations, they can also provide a common language which can facilitate difficult meetings or contacts. As Lord Carrington, the former Foreign Secretary (1979–82), remembered: 'I noticed how the art collection had enhanced the Embassies I visited and the discussions that the pictures provoked.'[18]

fig.37
Elisabeth Frink
Horse and Rider, 1969
Bronze

The idea that art is universal and can serve as a facilitator and a way into other conversations is picked up by the ambassador in Buenos Aires, Shan Morgan:

> The GAC artworks add a sense of history and offer useful talking points for guests. I find people comment most often on the Alan Davie tapestry [*Flag Walk*]… For me, this is the most important artwork as it gives a sense of a vibrant, modern Britain alongside the traditions of the past. The Elisabeth Frink *Horse and Rider* in the garden (fig.37), which

commemorates the reopening of diplomatic relations after
the Falklands conflict, is always a positive talking point...[19]

Given the geographical reach of the GAC and the display of the
Collection in non-gallery environments (many of them domestic
interiors), it follows that there is a range of unique logistical challenges.
A robust audit trail of all works of art has been established, with
regular inventory checks of works in the UK and abroad – as well as
a programme of visits abroad – as budgets allow. In this connection,
and given the absence of a daily curatorial presence, we also need to
take into account conservation requirements and the durability of works.
We may often admire an artist's output but are unable to acquire an
example until we find precisely the right work – one that will stand up
to the rigorous physical demands that will inevitably be made on it.
We have even developed a method with a conservator to protect works
when on display in a tropical climate and – as far as we know – ours is
the only collection that does this. Equally, subject matter can often
prevent us purchasing an artist's work: operating within central
government buildings, we have to be aware of possible political and
religious sensitivities.

The GAC's approach to the acquisition of works is distinct from that
of other public collections in a number of ways. The sheer number of
spaces in which we exhibit works of art, from high-profile, internationally
recognised buildings to functional conference rooms, coupled with the
limitations of the budget (£194,000 in 2010), means that the Collection
spans both major original works and lower value multiple prints. Despite
budgetary constraints, we are constantly looking for possible additions
to the Collection so we can promote up-to-date work in government
buildings. I've already explained that we buy works with connections
but we also make many purchases simply because they are strong in
their own right and demonstrate the creativity of British art and artists.
In addition to purchasing works (through dealers, galleries, artists,
auction rooms), we occasionally commission pieces (as distinct from
commissions for new buildings). For example, in 2010 Donald Urquhart
made one of his elegant black ink drawings *An Alphabet of LA*, wittily
matching Hollywood legends and places to each letter of the alphabet,
for display in the consul-general's residence in Los Angeles (fig.38).

The majority of purchases are of art made in recent years, although
we aim to add a significant historical work as well as a modern/
contemporary piece by a well-established artist each year. Approval
for GAC acquisitions is given by an Advisory Committee, a group with
an impressive range of expertise who also advise on the stewardship
of the Collection. I am fortunate to have had the wise counsel of two
chairmen, Sir John Tusa (1993–2003) and Julia Somerville (from 2003).

fig.38
Donald Urquhart
An Alphabet of LA, 2010
Ink on paper

The knowledge and experience of committee members has also been invaluable and Richard Dorment, art critic of the *Daily Telegraph* and a former member, gives his personal insight into the role of the committee in chapter 3.

Much has changed since 1998 when the BBC chose to call their documentary about the GAC *The Secret Art of Government*. For more than ten years, the GAC has been welcoming members of the public to our premises through the Open House Weekend scheme and giving regular public tours. The Collection has been online since 2001. This has provided easy access to the range of the GAC holdings and doubled the number of exhibition loan requests we receive. In 2011 the GAC is staging its first ever exhibition in a public gallery. This will undoubtedly bring welcome attention to the GAC's work and increase the public's understanding of what the GAC does and its value.

The Collection overall is a fascinating entity, all the more so for the histories of the works within it, from their creation to their acquisition, through to their display and reception. Across the world, the Collection is presented to an enormously broad range of people in unexpected ways and surprising locations (fig.39). Certain works have been in a single location for many years, while others have travelled more widely. In whatever context they are encountered – be it a minister's office, an ambassador's residence or the State Reception Rooms of 10 Downing Street – they introduce visual stimulation and additional points of interest which in turn contribute to the promotion of Britain and the creative talent it nurtures. Thanks to the capacity of art to transcend barriers, engage, amuse, entertain and inform, the GAC both captures and promotes the vital contribution of artists to defining Britain and its identity. More than a century into the Collection's life, this is now being more widely acknowledged, and I look forward with anticipation to seeing it grow not only in terms of scope, but also in impact and profile.

fig.39
Reception with portrait of *Queen Elizabeth II* by **Andy Warhol**, Residence of Deputy Permanent Representative to the United Nations, New York, January 2008

NOTES

1. Author's correspondence with Jack Straw, 22 September 2010.
2. Author's correspondence with George Osborne, 1 November 2010.
3. Text from speech made by David Lammy, summer 2005.
4. Correspondence between Paul Boateng and Julia Toffolo, GAC, 5 December 2007.
5. Author's correspondence with Jeremy Hunt, 22 October 2010.
6. Author's correspondence with Malcolm Rifkind, 25 August 2010.
7. Author's correspondence with Sir David Madden, 21 February 2002.
8. Author's correspondence with Sir John Sawers, 7 February 2008.
9. Author's correspondence with Sir Alan Collins, 14 February 2008.
10. Author's correspondence with Sir Mark Lyall-Grant, 18 September 2010.
11. Author's correspondence with Sir Peter Westmacott, 27 September 2010.
12. Wanjiru Hinga quoted in author's correspondence with Sir Rob Macaire, high commissioner, Kenya, 5 October 2010.
13. Author's correspondence with Teresa Albor, 15 September 2010.
14. Author's correspondence with Boyd McCleary, 23 August 2010.
15. Jenoliya David quoted in author's correspondence with Peter Hayes, high commissioner, Sri Lanka, 27 September 2010.
16. Author's correspondence with Sir Michael Arthur 29 November 2007.
17. Author's correspondence with Judith MacGregor, 29 September 2010.
18. Author's correspondence with Lord Carrington, 31 August 2010.
19. Author's correspondence with Shan Morgan, 14 September 2010.

fig.40
Edward Lear
View of Beirut, c.1861
Oil on canvas

fig.41
William Hogarth
*Unknown Gentleman in a Green
Velvet Cap, c.1740–45*
Oil on canvas

fig.42
John Constable
*Jane Anne Inglis (née Mason),
c.1808*
Oil on canvas

fig.43
Alexis-Simon Belle
*Prince James Francis Edward Stuart
('The Old Pretender') (1688–1766)
Jacobite claimant to the thrones
of England, Scotland, and Ireland,
c.1712*
Oil on canvas

2. SILENT WITNESSES: A BRIEF HISTORY OF THE GOVERNMENT ART COLLECTION

Julia Toffolo

[I] was present at the signing of the Russo-Polish treaty in the Secretary of State's room at the Foreign Office. It was signed against a background of spotlights and a foreground of cameramen by the P.M., Eden, Sikorski and Maisky, while a bust of the Younger Pitt looked down, rather disapprovingly I thought.
– John Colville, 30 July 1941[1]

In the absence of a revolution which would have made the Royal Collection available, until the first decades of the 20th century finding suitable works of art for display in Downing Street, ministerial departments and British missions abroad was a haphazard affair. Unlike other British national collections, the Government Art Collection came about not with the fanfare of an Act of Parliament, but instead as a series of faltering steps in response to this need. Clearly, art was required for such prestigious buildings, not only as decoration, but also to project an image commensurate with the surroundings, the history of the buildings and those who occupied them, and to help create a favourable image of Britain. Where were such works of art to come from? By and large, the occupants of such buildings were expected to fend for themselves, just as the millionaire art collector Robert Walpole, the first occupant of 10 Downing Street as 'First Lord of the Treasury' had done when he exhibited a portion of his own extensive art collection in that official residence in the 1730s. At a time when the landowning aristocracy for the most part formed the governing class, this was an economical, if unpredictable, solution.

The only officially supplied art in government buildings abroad took the form of royal portraits copied from the originals owned by the monarch. A large copy of George Hayter's portrait of Queen Victoria, sent to St Petersburg in the 1860s, was casting a regal air of authority over the British embassy when it was stormed by Bolshevik forces in 1918 and the British naval attaché Captain Cromie shot dead. This and the other royal portraits there were subsequently moved to the new embassy in Moscow after the city reverted to being the Russian capital following the Russian Revolution, the strong physical similarity between the portrait of King George V and the dead Czar Nicholas II reportedly sometimes causing confusion for Russian guests.

Lord Halifax arrives as British ambassador with his wife Lady Halifax at the recently constructed British embassy in Washington, DC, in January 1941, walking past one of the standard royal portraits of *King George V* hung on the Staircase.

In a piecemeal fashion, individual government departments and buildings gradually acquired works by purchase, loan or gift. After the signature of the Treaty of Locarno with Germany at the Foreign Office in London in December 1925, to fit with the grandeur and dignity of the surroundings a concerted effort was made to acquire portraits of past Foreign Secretaries for display in what subsequently became known as the 'Locarno Room'. In response Lord Londonderry[2] presented a copy of the original portrait of his ancestor Lord Castlereagh by Thomas Lawrence, which he had lent for the event.[3] In 1929 the chief constables of the Metropolitan Police presented a full-length portrait of their founder Sir Robert Peel, to be hung in the main reception room of the Home Office (then located on Whitehall). And at the British embassy in Cairo, portraits were acquired of suitable figures associated with the history of the British in Egypt – those of Lord Kitchener, Lord Cromer and Sir Eldon Gorst were acquired by gift from various sources in 1927 and 1928. Acknowledging the donation of the Gorst portrait, Sir Lionel Earle, Permanent Secretary at the Office of Works, wrote:

> I know well how much portraits of past holders of the post add to the interest and appearance of diplomatic buildings, and in these days when diplomats are transferred so frequently from one post to another I realise the difficulties they meet with very often in furnishing the walls of the buildings in the manner worthy of the representatives of His Majesty abroad, particularly as no pictures or other ornaments are permitted to be provided from my Department's funds. It is, therefore, on gifts such as yours and on the private purse of the head of the mission that we have to rely for anything, such as pictures, which go to make the interior of the buildings interesting and attractive.[4]

Two portraits of King George III and Queen Charlotte (after the originals by Allan Ramsay) were donated by Lord Duveen in 1937 and sent out to Sir Edwin Lutyens's newly built embassy in Washington in 1938. However, at the ambassador's request, they were installed on the staircase, but only at a time in the year when Washington society had least opportunity to notice the symbolic presence of the 'tyrant' King George in the house.[5]

There was extensive reliance upon loans of works of art from national and private sources for display in government buildings, but this proved no real long-term solution without an overall strategy with regard to style or quality. This was seen in the British embassy in Paris where, for example, the Royal Collection was prevailed upon to provide some loans, but the quality of these – perhaps surprisingly – was very uneven.[6] The Prime Minister's and the Chancellor of the Exchequer's residences at

'The Big Four' at 10 Downing Street: Prime Minister Andrew Bonar Law at a meeting to discuss reparations and Allied debts after World War I with Prime Minister Raymond Poincaré of France, Prime Minister Benito Mussolini of Italy and Prime Minister Georges Theunis of Belgium, December 1922. The meeting took place in the main drawing room (Pillared Room) with a large portrait of *Richard Weston, 1st Earl of Portland (1577–1635)* in the background, displayed for many decades at Number 10.

10 and 11 Downing Street also relied heavily on loans from national collections. However, by the end of the 19th century, a small group of portraits of relevant political figures (of unknown provenance) was being shown in Number 10. In the early 20th century, several copies of portraits of historical luminaries such as Nelson, Pitt, Wellington, Fox and Burke were donated to 10 Downing Street, as well as a set of portrait prints of former Prime Ministers which have hung on the Staircase ever since.

A head-and-shoulders portrait of Robert Walpole was donated to Number 10 in the early years of the century by Lord Lee of Fareham (who also gave Chequers to the Prime Minister for use as a country residence). This has hung above the fireplace in the Cabinet Room at 10 Downing Street ever since, witnessing not only every Cabinet meeting held in the room, but a number of highly significant historical moments as well, including Neville Chamberlain's declaration of war against Germany on 3 September 1939, the signing of the Anglo-Polish Treaty on 5 August 1940[7] and Churchill's VE Day broadcast on 8 May 1945. The presence of this portrait, just above the Prime Minister's chair, has become highly symbolic, as Peter Hennessy has remarked in his book on British Prime Ministers: '… that seat beneath that portrait in that room remains the ultimate prize for which the politically ambitious strive in Britain.'[8]

Some ambassadors resorted to acquiring works of art themselves for their posts. Lord D'Abernon, ambassador to Germany from 1920 to 1926,[9] purchased in Berlin two decorative paintings by 17th-century Dutch and Flemish masters to be hung in the embassy. Suggesting that this might permanently solve the problems of how to fill the spaces on some of the walls, he sold them to the British government in 1924.[10] In the following decade and a half, these paintings witnessed official receptions and dinners, visits by prominent members of the National Socialist government and grand receptions during the 1936 Olympic Games before presumed destruction in the building during World War II.

As premiers, ministers and diplomats increasingly came from less wealthy backgrounds,[11] without personal collections of works to hand or the money to buy them, it gradually became apparent that piecemeal efforts to acquire works of art for display in major government buildings were no longer either appropriate or effective. There was no real long-term solution to all of these issues other than for public money to fill the breach, and in 1898 the Treasury authorised the Office of Works to purchase works of art for government buildings and to act as a central body to care for what had already been acquired for them. This was regularised in 1907 with an annual sum of £300 for making purchases or commissioning copies of portraits for 'the decoration of rooms in public buildings and offices',[12] the larger the better, since this would 'save a good sum in decoration'.[13] With an apparent emphasis on the acquisition of 'worthy' subjects suitable for display in grand Whitehall buildings, this money was spent mostly on portraits in the early years, including those of William Kent (purchased 1915), King Charles II (purchased 1900) and King James II (purchased 1907), with a very occasional foray into relevant landscapes such as a *View in St James's Park* by an unknown artist (purchased 1929).

However, such funds were intended only for the acquisition of art for government buildings in London. By the 1930s concerns began to emerge about the need to increase British prestige in government buildings abroad, especially as, to the despair of many contemporaries, the rising German and Italian dictatorships evidently better understood the importance of promoting their image abroad than the British, and had no qualms about spending money in order to do so. Sir Nevile Henderson, who served as ambassador to Belgrade, Buenos Aires and finally Berlin, was under no illusions about the matter:

> It is a small thing, but prestige is worth cultivating and has its value and even a few more such portraits would add distinction to what is, I regret to say, a shoddy affair, the Embassy House at Buenos Aires. Mussolini is no fool and there is sense and foresight behind the new Italian Embassies and

fig.44
Cultural diplomacy: Augustus John's portrait of *Edgar Vincent, Viscount d'Abernon (1857–1941)* when ambassador to Berlin, *c*.1925–26.

Legations which he stole from Austria or has since created. In Belgrade this was noticeable and I find the same thing here where the Italian Embassy is far the best at Buenos Aires (not the biggest for the ugly and pretentious U.S. Embassy is that).[14]

Henderson also commented in letters and his autobiography on how the parsimony of the British Treasury was damaging British influence overseas. It was simply no longer good enough to rely on the possessions and good taste (or otherwise) of incoming ambassadors:[15]

> … in peace-time it is the hardest thing in the world to get the Treasury to spend money abroad. Our parsimony in this respect is in glaring contrast to what poorer countries such as the French, Italians or Germans are used to spend on any purpose calculated to increase their prestige or serve as propaganda.[16]

In a move that can be seen in some small way as a form of 'cultural rearmament' in government buildings abroad, in 1935 the Treasury sanctioned an annual grant of £250 as a Picture Fund to be spent on acquiring works of art for British missions, 'making our embassies in the principal European capitals more worthy than they are at present'.[17] A Picture Committee was established to acquire suitable works – which wherever possible should be British – and analyse where they might best be placed in these important representational spaces. Additionally, the National Galleries (Overseas Loans) Act of the same year enabled the national collections to lend more works of art from their holdings to government buildings abroad. What the legislation allowed them to lend, however (and, indeed, what they were prepared to lend), was extremely limited and over the years Government-owned works of art were increasingly used instead.

The development of a strategy for acquiring and exhibiting works of art in government buildings at home and abroad was clearly welcome, but it was to create a whole new set of challenges which the Collection still faces today. These include the need to respond to changes in taste and policy dictated by political considerations; the need to explore and exploit cultural diplomatic links all over the world; and the need to operate in often demanding international circumstances completely outside the Collection's control.

In the years leading up to the outbreak of World War II moves were made to fill obvious gaps in the picture hang in diplomatic missions, if possible with works displaying notable links with the countries in which they were located, a policy that has been followed ever since. Following the visit to Paris in June 1935 of the First Commissioner of Works and his subsequent report on his findings, a portrait of the 1st Duke of Wellington was purchased (he had acquired the British embassy building in 1814), and a portrait of Sir Robert Murray Keith, British minister to Denmark, for Copenhagen. A marble bust of Stratford Canning, Viscount Stratford de Redcliffe, British ambassador to the Ottoman Empire, was sent to Istanbul in 1935. Works of general interest were also acquired, with a portrait of Master Stenninge by Mason Chamberlin sent out to Athens soon after its purchase in 1936. Sir Nevile Henderson's persistence paid off, for in 1936 he received for display in Buenos Aires one of the first pictures purchased from the Picture Fund – a large landscape by Viviano Codazzi of the Arch of Constantine. All of these works remain in these same locations today, testifying to their long-term suitability for the posts concerned.

At home, a bust of William Pitt the Younger was acquired for the Foreign Secretary's room in the Foreign Office. Pitt's haughty presence has inhabited the room ever since, witnessing many meetings and treaty signings over the course of the last seven decades.[18] As Chancellor of the Exchequer from 1937 to 1940, Sir John Simon was keen to transform his office in the Treasury (the Treasury Board Room, now Cabinet Office Conference Room A at 70 Whitehall) with a coherent series of portraits of former Chancellors, including another bust of that perennial favourite William Pitt the Younger which the Office of Works had purchased for the purpose in 1937. Meanwhile, a copy of the Pre-Raphaelite artist John Everett Millais's portrait of William Gladstone – donated in 1895 (and still at Number 11) – was hung on the wall opposite John Simon's desk in the Study at 11 Downing Street.

By the late 1930s, despite mounting international security concerns, there were increasing demands for works of art in British missions, demands that could not be met due to insufficient funding, which may in some cases have been fortuitous in the long run. In 1937, Sir Robert Craigie, British ambassador in Tokyo, was particularly keen to obtain pictures to assist his diplomatic efforts, on the basis that: 'Anglo-Japanese relationships are not too happy at present and, as part of the effort to wean the Japanese from German influence, it will be desirable that a good deal of social activity takes place at the British Embassy'.[19] A year later the ambassador wrote to say that he was unable to understand why he could not secure art for Tokyo when Mussolini, by contrast, had agreed to send valuable Italian masterpieces for display in the new Italian Culture Hall to be built in the city. 'Is it the fear of air-raids?' he queried. 'If so, I wonder whether they are really justified in thinking that the danger of an air-raid is greater in Tokyo than it is in any capital in Europe today, not excluding London!'[20] Fortunately the paintings sent out to Paris, Copenhagen and Athens in the 1930s were

Two Chancellors: Chancellor of the Exchequer Sir John Simon in the Treasury Board Room (later Cabinet Room A in the Cabinet Office, 70 Whitehall) in a photograph taken by Cecil Beaton in 1940. A sculpture of *William Pitt the Younger*, purchased in June 1937, is in the background on a specially made new plinth.

not damaged during the war, for although these buildings were abandoned for periods of the war, they were not bombed, and their contents remained intact.

It was after several paintings in the Chancellor of the Exchequer's office in the Treasury had been damaged by bombing in October 1940 (including a portrait of William Lowndes that had been acquired by HM Treasury in 1925), a blast which also affected Number 10, that the Prime Minister Winston Churchill asked for art at 10 Downing Street to be removed to a place of safety. Bombs fell near to Number 10 again on 20 February 1944, affecting several historic portraits on show in the main drawing room, known as the Pillared Room. After removal from Number 10 these portraits were exhibited in Conference Room B of the War Cabinet Rooms (nowadays occupied by HM Treasury) for the Dominion Prime Ministers' Conference of May 1944, before being returned to Number 10.

At the outbreak of war: Members of Neville Chamberlain's War Cabinet pose for an official photograph in the State Dining Room of 10 Downing Street, November 1939. In the background to the right hangs Hubert von Herkomer's copy portrait of Prime Minister the *3rd Marquess of Salisbury (1830–1903)*, donated to Number 10 in 1912.

London can take it: Bomb damage in the Pillared Room, 10 Downing Street, 21 February 1944. From left to right are portraits of *Spencer Perceval*, *Henry Pelham* and *Henry Booth, 1st Earl of Warrington*, with early 18th-century furniture in the style of William Kent.

Acquisitions continued to be made in a small way during the war. In 1942 C. R. W. Nevinson presented Churchill with a new painting imbued with symbolism, *Battlefields of Britain*, which Churchill accepted on behalf of the nation. At the same time, the Ministry of Information oversaw a scheme to commission artists in the field to record events in the theatre of war: some 200 of these works by artists such as Carel Weight and Edward Bawden entered the Collection after the conflict was over.[21]

The acquisition of art for government buildings began in earnest after 1945. The Picture Committee reconvened, with additional funds to spend, the Government now recognising that a proper strategy to acquire a 'repository' of pictures especially for use by heads of mission abroad was required. A part-time curator was appointed (Richard Walker served in this capacity for 30 years) and a basic inventory compiled. Works for the repository were acquired by purchase and, as before, by gift and loan (via a series of public appeals), the quality of some of these continuing to be uneven. The Ministry of Works also took advantage of the large number of country house sales after the war in order to acquire both portraits and landscapes.[22]

In contrast to the 1930s, when the display of modern art in missions abroad – even when offered as a gift – was rejected as 'giving rise to undesirable controversy',[23] for the first time the Picture Committee and the Government advocated the acquisition of contemporary art. This was coupled with a new emphasis on acquiring works to be shown overseas in order to promote Britain and British cultural endeavour, a responsibility the Government Art Collection (GAC) still very much carries today. Early purchases included works by Ivon Hitchens and John Nash, while relatively cheaper prints and watercolours began to be collected in large numbers to fill walls as economically as possible. Early forays into commissioning work abroad included an important group of five paintings by John Piper for the British embassy in Rio de Janeiro.[24] Post-war austerity meant that public funds had to be supplemented, so in 1951 David Eccles as Minister of Works established a special subscription fund to acquire items for the Collection (accounting for some 400 historical and modern works) and these funds were also used to commission a group of works to celebrate the coronation of Queen Elizabeth II in 1953. L. S. Lowry was included in this latter enterprise, producing a unique take on the artistic constraints of the subject matter in his *The Procession passing the Queen Victoria Memorial*. A few years earlier, Lowry's painting *Lancashire Fair: Good Friday, Daisy Nook* had been purchased and was subsequently to become a recurring favourite among Prime Ministers. Harold Wilson chose it for his new study at 10 Downing Street in 1968, and it has spent most of its history since that time at Number 10, Margaret Thatcher displaying it in the Prime Minister's flat. At the time

The shape of things to come:
A portrait of *Winston Churchill* by Julian Lamar, donated to the British embassy in Washington in 1943, dominates an embassy meeting of 1947 or 1948 attended by (on the left) second secretary Nicholas Henderson, later ambassador to Warsaw, Paris and Washington. The as yet unexposed spy Donald Maclean, then first secretary, sits on the desk.

fig.45
A favourite guest at Number 10:
Lancashire Fair: Good Friday, Daisy Nook by L. S. Lowry, painted in 1946 and acquired by the Ministry of Works in 1947.

of writing, the painting hangs at the top of the staircase, where it can be clearly seen by all visitors to Number 10.

In the 1950s, funds for the acquisition of works of art increased, and the Ministry of Works made some astute and important purchases with international connections that could be exploited in host countries. These included three 1860s landscapes of Ceylon by Edward Lear and a famous portrait of Lord Byron by Thomas Phillips which have spent most of their history since acquisition in Colombo and Athens respectively. In 1951 full-length portraits of Frederick and Elizabeth of Bohemia were purchased for the historic embassy building in Prague in response to the ambassador's request for examples of Czech–British connections, and are still located there.

In 1952 the Marquis of Salisbury, Secretary of State for Commonwealth

Changing times: Prime Minister Anthony Eden welcomes Egyptian President Nasser to the ambassador's residence in Cairo, January 1955, in front of a reminder of Britain's historical influence in Egypt, a portrait of Evelyn Baring, 1st Earl of Cromer (1841–1917), later temporarily removed from display.

Relations, felt that Britain needed to maintain a high level of artistic representation in the countries of the British Empire that were gradually becoming independent:

> I know how anxious you are that the houses of our representative abroad should have pictures worthily representing British art, and I think you will agree that this is even more important in the other main Commonwealth capitals than in many foreign capitals. Our future prestige and influence in the rest of the Commonwealth largely depends on retaining respect for British standards and traditions and our High Commissioner's [sic] houses must be the centre of such influence in each country… Australia has a lively school of contemporary painting of its own and Australian taste is developing rapidly. We cannot therefore expect to hold their respect with anything second rate: on the other hand, if we can have a few really good specimens of British painting, this will yield real dividends in countering the school of thought that is inclined to look increasingly to America and to write Britain off as a spent force. While we naturally don't want to enter into a decorative race with America, we happen to have an opportunity in Canberra to make an effective contrast since the large new U.S. embassy there is, we are told by our people, filled with bad modern American stuff….'[25]

In other parts of the world, Britain's declining international status brought new challenges to the Collection and those responsible for it as the symbolic meaning of some works of art in buildings changed over the years. Prime Minister Anthony Eden was photographed with President Nasser in front of the portrait of Lord Cromer at the ambassador's residence in Cairo in 1955, but when diplomatic relations were restored in 1961 after the Suez crisis, it was thought politic to remove this and the other portraits that had been acquired in the early years of the century to celebrate the British presence in Egypt, but which were by then felt to have 'imperialist' connotations.[26]

…it seems to me that the showing made by the houses and indeed the gardens of Her Majesty's Missions abroad is a matter of real importance from the point of view of the standing that we may hope to enjoy in the eyes of foreign peoples. And on this standing, I venture to submit, will depend not only the respect in which we are held, but also the willingness of other nations to buy from us those skills which we must export if we are to pay our way in the world of today.
– Nigel Ronald, British ambassador to Lisbon, July 1952[27]

A new image of Britain: the main reception room of the newly built ambassador's residence in Warsaw, making news in 1964. Joan Eardley's large energetic painting *The Sea No. III* (1963) dominates the far wall in a resolutely modernist interior with contemporary furniture.

Post-war Soviet Bloc countries presented other forms of challenge for the Collection, including security issues, difficult environmental surroundings[28] and the choice of appropriate works. In the early 1960s a group of contemporary works and a small group of 18th-century naval paintings of the Caribbean (including, topically, a view of *The Capture of Havana by the English Squadron* by Dominic Serres) were dispatched for hanging in the historic interior of the British embassy in Moscow. Simultaneously the Collection worked closely with the Foreign Office to provide contemporary works of art for display in the new residence in Warsaw, an unashamedly modernist building designed to project the image of a 'new Britain' abroad – a hang that did not however survive the more conservative tastes of successive ambassadors.

Back in the UK, the GAC responded to the needs of incoming political administrations. A pattern began to emerge that continues to underpin the Collection's activities and holdings to this day – to reflect at home and abroad the changing priorities and tastes of particular governments and their individual members. Under the premiership of Harold Wilson, the official display of works of art in some of the reception areas at Number 10 began for the first time to show evidence of the political and cultural preferences of the incumbent Prime Minister. This was in contrast to the static, historical hangs designed to suit the political role of the building, as had previously been the case. In the mid-1960s,

'... with only the melancholy portrait of Robert Walpole for company': Harold Wilson works in the Cabinet Room at 10 Downing Street in the early months of his first term of government, October 1964.

with Britain becoming a nation less deferential to tradition, Harold and Mary Wilson invited many non-Establishment guests including show business personalities to official events. In the same way they were keen to be associated with modern British art, and displayed works by younger artists such as Robert Medley, Keith Vaughan and Henry Inlander along the first-floor corridor. Similarly, following Minister for the Arts Jennie Lee's 1965 White Paper on the arts, the Collection began to purchase a large number of prints by contemporary young British artists for display in government buildings in the UK.

In 1968 a first-floor room at Number 10 that had intermittently served as a private area for the Prime Minister was converted into a study for Harold Wilson. Prior to this Wilson had worked alone in the Cabinet Room downstairs, 'with only the melancholy portrait of Robert Walpole for company'.[29] As well as requesting Lowry's *Lancashire Fair* for his study, Wilson revealed a particular liking for a newly purchased painting by Daphne Reynolds, *The Watcher*, a painting which, like the Lowry, hung in the study during both his administrations.[30] With hindsight it is tempting to attribute Wilson's choice of a work of art with a title and

Man of the people: Harold Wilson lights up in his new Study at 10 Downing Street, *c.*1969, with Lowry's *Lancashire Fair: Good Friday, Daisy Nook* behind. Government buildings have never offered ideal museum-type environments.

fig.46
View from the top: *Westminster II*
by William Coldstream, 1974.
One of several paintings Coldstream
took the opportunity to make of
the view from Room 1702 in one
of the towers of the brutalist
Department of the Environment
building at Great Marsham Street
while serving as a member of the
GAC's Advisory Committee.

composition such as this[31] to his concerns that a portrait in 10 Downing
Street was wired for sound by the security services.[32]

**Is that man crazy? He thinks there's a bug behind
all the pictures.**
– George H. W. Bush, director of the CIA, after
visiting Harold Wilson in Number 10 during Wilson's
second Premiership.[33]

By contrast, Wilson's Conservative successor Edward Heath wanted
to project a grandiose, traditional and more international style. Heath
banished from the State Dining Room the early 20th-century copy
portraits of famous British historical figures that had been there for
decades and relied upon loans from private and foreign sources of
paintings by 18th-century masters and Auguste Renoir.[34] This situation
was in turn quickly reversed when Wilson replaced Heath in 1974.

In the 1970s the Department of the Environment took over the Ministry
of Works (and thus responsibility for the Collection); greater purchasing
power enabled continued acquisition of modern and historical works,
as well as reinstating the Collection's role of commissioning works of art
for the Government. The first such commission, in 1979, was a sculpture
by Ian Hamilton Finlay – *Sundial*, for the garden of the ambassador's

Special occasion: To celebrate the 250th anniversary of 10 Downing Street, Margaret Thatcher poses with H. M. The Queen and all surviving Prime Ministers in the White Room of Number 10, 4 December 1985. Behind them is Winston Churchill's *Seascape*, which had been purchased in 1984 at Mrs Thatcher's request.

residence in Bonn. In 1980 the Collection became part of the Office of Arts and Libraries and acquired its current name – Government Art Collection – in 1981, Dr Wendy Baron having taken over as the organisation's head in 1978.

Margaret Thatcher's eagerness to celebrate Britain's position in the world and reverse a perceived international decline was reflected in the art she wished to exhibit at Number 10. She was also keen to remodel the appearance of Number 10 itself, redecorating three of the upstairs reception rooms of the house in a more ornate interpretation of 18th-century classicism. Fully understanding the building's potential as an international showcase for Britain, she wanted to establish displays of 'British worthies', largely through loans from private national sources, a practice which brought criticism in the press and among politicians.[35] In this connection in the early 1980s Margaret Thatcher encouraged the GAC to purchase a 1920s painting by Winston Churchill, *Seascape*, which during the rest of her premiership hung in her study, in her flat, or in the White Room at Number 10.

As in World War II, the location of so many works of art in buildings all over the world occasionally makes them vulnerable to potential threats beyond the Collection's control, threats which the Ministry of Works and its successors have always had little choice but to tolerate for the greater purpose of projecting the UK abroad. The 1980s brought new examples of these challenges. Nothing happened to the works of art in the residences in Buenos Aires during the Falklands crisis in 1982 or in Kuwait in 1990 following the Iraqi invasion but, in contrast, during the anarchy in Bucharest in the days leading up to the arrest and execution of Nicolae Ceausescu and his wife in December 1989 the British embassy was stormed and damaged by rioters. Six pictures were destroyed in the resulting fire and several others damaged: three of the works on show today in the (replacement) residence in Bucharest were scarred by gunfire. Works of art were returned to the UK following a fire at the British consulate-general in Istanbul (the historic 19th-century Pera House) in 1999. However, six watercolours of views of the Crimean War by William Simpson remained in the consul-general's temporary office, at his request, while Pera House was being repaired. In a bomb attack in November 2003 he and his secretary were killed and the room's contents destroyed.

Dangers have sometimes been closer to home. On 7 February 1991 an IRA mortar bomb exploded in the garden at Number 10 while John Major's Cabinet was in session in the Cabinet Room, shattering the windows on the garden side of Downing Street and of the nearby Cabinet Office. The 1980s-installed plaster ceiling in the White Room of Number 10 was damaged although, miraculously, no actual works of art at 10, 11 or 12 Downing Street were harmed. The one work that was damaged – penetrated by shrapnel from the blast – was the double portrait *Henry Pelham and his Secretary John Roberts* by John Shackleton, a painting for many years displayed in the historic Conference Room A of William Kent's Treasury building (now the Cabinet Office) – the same room where paintings had been damaged in the Blitz of October 1940. The following decade saw investment to strengthen the security of the architecture of these buildings, each refurbishment episode requiring the GAC to remove and then to reinstall the hundreds of works of art on show.

From May 1997 the GAC underwent more changes following the beginning of the New Labour era and the (coincidental) arrival of a new GAC director, Penny Johnson (the directorship of the GAC has never been a political appointment, unlike its American counterpart, the Art in Embassies Program). The GAC became part of the new Department for Culture, Media and Sport (having come under the umbrella of the Department of National Heritage in 1992), and over the following years was to gain from increases in budgets and staffing levels as the demands upon its services grew due to the frequency of new displays and a much greater commissioning role.

In his jungle: Deputy Prime Minister Michael Heseltine in his office in the Cabinet Office, 70 Whitehall in 1996. Peter Tillemans's huge *View of the Thames from Richmond Hill* provides a suitably grand 18th-century backdrop.

67

While art displayed in ministers' offices serves to promote Britain, it also enables government ministers themselves to demonstrate to staff and visitors that a new person has arrived in office. Nigel Lawson made his mark in this way during his first days in office after becoming Secretary of State for Energy in 1981:

> I… put in pride of place on one of the walls the large 18th-century portrait of Henry Pelham which I had in my room at the Treasury… there was no harm in letting the Department know right from the start that they had not merely a new Secretary of State, but a new broom.[36]

With the new Labour government, this tradition continued: whether they had a genuine appreciation for it or not, following the General Election of May 1997 the vast majority of New Labour ministers chose 20th-century and contemporary art to replace the (generally) more traditional art they encountered on their walls when they took up office. The cultural shift brought about by the new government and ministerial changes were the subject of a BBC TV documentary shot in 1997–98 with the intriguing – if not wholly accurate – title *The Secret Art of Government*.

Gradually the GAC introduced more contemporary art into 10 Downing Street, at first mostly through loans, but little by little through its own acquisitions, partly to fill gaps created by reduced funding for the Collection in the 1980s when comparatively few purchases could be made. Other gaps were filled by acquiring and exhibiting work by female artists and depicting female sitters, in contrast to the male-dominated displays the new government had inherited. The Collection briefly became associated with New Labour's push towards the cultural phenomenon known as 'Cool Britannia', showing modern and contemporary work at the November 1997 British–French Summit at Canary Wharf and at the European Summit held at Lancaster House in 1998. It also organised the first strategic showing of British contemporary art in the Glazed Galleries of the ambassador's residence in Paris – an initiative that has since become a regular fixture. Building on the success in Paris, contemporary work has also been displayed to great effect in the historic interiors of the residences in Vienna, Washington, Berlin, Tokyo and New Delhi; while working with the Foreign and Commonwealth Office (FCO) the GAC has commissioned new art for the many new office buildings erected by the FCO since 1997, including those in Berlin, Moscow, Colombo, Chennai, Doha, Sana'a and Madrid. What may prove (owing to scarcity of resources in the future) to be the high-water mark of the GAC's commissions in the UK was the exterior façade and street-based works of art for Terry Farrell's new Home Office building on Marsham Street, completed in 2005.

An admirer of Winston Churchill:
President George W. Bush with
British ambassador to the USA
Sir Christopher Meyer in the
Oval Office of the White House,
Washington, DC, July 2001. Despite
reports to the contrary, the GAC's
bust by Jacob Epstein was always a
loan and never a gift.

The GAC's role as guardian of the Government's own collection of works of art has over the years occasionally placed it symbolically at the coalface of international relations and their political repercussions. In 2001, in response to a remark made by President George W. Bush about his admiration for Winston Churchill, Tony Blair asked the GAC to provide a likeness of the great man for display in the Oval Office of the White House. Accordingly, continuing its policy of showing art with important cultural and artistic links outside the UK, the GAC lent one of its two bronze busts by Jacob Epstein. The loan, which was understood from the start to be only for the duration of Bush's presidency, caused much national and international interest and criticism in the British and American press, giving rise to demands from some parties that the bust be returned to the UK. (The loan continued as agreed until January 2009.)

The UK's close relationship with the USA over the Iraq War provided an example of how works of art can acquire a new significance for those familiar with them. In December 1999 the GAC had placed a large 1950s painting by Richard Eurich, *Coast Scene with Rainbow*, in the Prime Minister's personal office (or 'den') at Number 10, the very heart of Blair's 'sofa' government. There this nostalgic evocation of the artist's childhood memories of the English coast became the physical background to the many discussions held in the room over the British government's decision to go to war with Iraq in 2003.

A moment in time: World War I veterans Bill Stone (aged 108), Henry Allingham (112) and Harry Patch (110) in the Pillared Room at 10 Downing Street on the 90th anniversary of the end of that war, 11 November 2008. Behind them are portraits of *Sarah Churchill, Duchess of Marlborough, Queen Elizabeth I* and *Prince James Francis Edward Stuart ('The Old Pretender')*.

Some rooms in Whitehall buildings have undergone many changes of use during their long histories and have been decorated and redecorated in many styles, required to project a variety of different images and purposes. As always throughout its history, the GAC has had to provide – usually at very short notice – suitable works of art from its holdings that are in keeping with and emphasise each room's new use. In 2003 the Prime Minister's study at 10 Downing Street underwent yet another transformation, emerging after the 'makeover' as a minimalist meeting room. But in 2008 the same room was changed again, this time into an 18th-century-style library interior, and as such was subsequently extensively used by Prime Minister Gordon Brown for public interviews. After both transformations GAC art was required to promote the room's new function.

Shortly after the General Election of 6 May 2010, which produced a hung Parliament, the end of the New Labour government was discussed in Gordon Brown's office at 12 Downing Street[37] ironically in front of Terry Frost's abstract *Suspended Forms*. Simultaneously, around the corner in the Cabinet Office, the historic Cabinet Room B was hosting talks between the Conservatives and Liberal Democrats towards forming the Coalition government. This large room, for many years a meeting room, had been converted for use as an office for the then Deputy Prime Minister Michael Heseltine in 1995 and hung with suitable 18th-century works. Subsequently used by a number of senior civil servants and ministers over the years with several associated changes of display, the Coalition talks took place in front of the contemporary pieces of art the GAC had provided for its previous occupant, Olympics Minister Tessa Jowell: two photographs of London by John Riddy and a large abstract work by Marta Marcé – *Untitled (MM733)* – inspired by a popular toy.

From its stuttering beginnings, the Collection now comprises some 13,500 works of fine art, with at least two-thirds on show at any one time in over 400 government buildings in the UK and around the world. These buildings enable the GAC to present its holdings in varied architectural environments ranging from historical and modern

Suspended Forms: Gordon Brown and his close advisors around Terry Frost's painting of this title in the Prime Minister's office next to the Number 10 Press Office at 12 Downing Street, shortly before Brown conceded defeat to the new Coalition government on 11 May 2010 and left Downing Street.

domestic interiors to contemporary office spaces, entrance halls and conference rooms. The Picture Committee – now known as the Advisory Committee on the Government Art Collection and expanded from its original small membership – continues to meet, and the GAC is still purchasing works for the Collection, which now embraces examples of most schools, genres and periods of British fine art from the early 16th century to the present day, ranging from early portraiture to video and neon art. Reliance upon public collections for loans and private individuals for donations has largely become a thing of the past, and a coherent strategy for the acquisition and display of works of art, in the national interest, is paramount. Despite a recurring press obsession with missing works of art,[38] the GAC's role in projecting British culture in important government buildings and supporting and promoting British artists should surely be regarded as a national success story.

Having been one of the first UK collections to acquire a computer database in the early 1980s, the GAC placed all its original works of art online as long ago as 2001. Added to this, the art in government buildings is seen by thousands of visitors, making – as it always has done – regular appearances in the background of press photographs, television news reports and documentaries. After 113 years, whatever the future may have in store for the Collection, it is surely not – and never has been – hidden from view.

New man at Number 10: Prime Minister David Cameron sits at the Cabinet table at 10 Downing Street in September 2010, echoing Harold Wilson's pose nearly half a century earlier. *Robert Walpole*, above, has seen it all before.

NOTES

1. John Colville, *The Fringes of Power: Downing Street Diaries 1939–1955* (London, 2004), p. 367, entry for 30 July 1941. Colville served as Winston Churchill's Assistant Private Secretary from 1940 to 1941 and from 1943 to 1945.
2. The 7th Marquess of Londonderry (1878–1949).
3. *The Times*, 10 March 1926. It was hoped that other current descendants of famous Foreign Secretaries of the past would make a similar gesture.
4. Letter, 17 February 1928, to Lady Sykes from Sir Lionel Earle, Permanent Secretary at the Office of Works, thanking her for the gift of the portrait of Sir Eldon Gorst for Cairo, GAC File AA 3005/1 Part 1.
5. Lord Halifax later recalled how his predecessor as ambassador Lord Lothian used these portraits as diplomatic tools: '[W]e were told that Lothian used to enjoy puzzling his guests from Congress by pointing out the picture as that of the Founder of the American Republic, and presently relieving their perplexed expression at seeing so unfamiliar a presentation of George Washington by gently adding, "King George III".' Lord Halifax, *Fullness of Days* (London, 1957), p. 239.
6. In 1928 two works by Franz Floris on loan from the Royal Collection were described as 'so indifferent… totally unworthy to hang in a house of the dignity of the embassy at Paris', GAC File AA 3025/1 Part 1.
7. 'A photographer, for the first time in history, took a photograph of the signatories in the Cabinet Room', John Colville, op. cit., pp. 173–174, entry for 5 August 1940.
8. Peter Hennessy, *The Prime Minister, the Office and its Holders since 1945* (London, 2000) p. 39.
9. In March 1925 Augustus John was personally invited by D'Abernon to stay at the embassy in Berlin prior to the Locarno Conference so as to make sketches and portraits of several important figures, amongst them D'Abernon himself. In 1985 the GAC purchased this portrait at auction, GAC16337.
10. National Archives, File T 161/76.
11. 'The modern ambassador is coming more and more to be the type of man who has not got, and cannot be expected to have, a large number of pictures of his own.' Letter to the Lord Chamberlain from Philip Sassoon, First Commissioner of Works, 7 July 1937 (asking for loans for the British embassy, Tokyo, from the Royal Collection), GAC File AA 3128/1 Part 1.
12. National Archives WORK 54/50, note from the Treasury to the First Commissioner of the Office of Works, 8 April 1907.
13. National Archives WORK 54/50, letter from Lord Esher, First Commissioner, Office of Works, to Francis Mowatt, Permanent Secretary of HM Treasury, 5 December 1899: £150 was thought sufficient for the purpose.
14. Sir Nevile Henderson, ambassador to Buenos Aires, to Sir Robert Vansittart, Permanent Under-Secretary, Foreign Office, 11 August 1936, GAC File AA3006/1 Part 1.
15. The quality of what was on display in important missions abroad was a matter for concern. In June 1935, W. Ormsby-Gore, first commissioner of works at the Office of Works 1931–6, remarked that the anteroom in the British embassy in Paris contained two small landscapes by Adriaen van Dienst and 'a very bad copy of *The Mystic Marriage of St Catherine* by Correggio in the Louvre. The unsuitability of this picture for the British embassy cannot be too strongly emphasised, and it should be removed altogether', GAC File AA 3025/1 Part 1. The situation in Vienna was no better: 'Sir Walford Selby has placed his own collection in the Legation. It consists of a few very bad and dirty old masters and a number of watercolour copies of Turner's oils, done by Sir Walford Selby's aunt. He is extremely proud of his collection and was hurt at the suggestion that anything should be lent from the National Gallery.' Kenneth Clark, director of the National Gallery, to W. Ormsby-Gore, 4 May 1936, GAC File AA3070/1 Part 1.
16. Nevile Henderson, *Water under the Bridges* (London, 1945), p. 142.
17. Letter from W. Ormsby-Gore to Sir John Simon (Foreign Office), 5 June 1934, GAC File AA 634/1 Part 1. The £250 was to include packing and transportation costs as well as purchase costs.
18. For example, see John Colville's remark at note 1.
19. Minute from Patrick Duff, Permanent Secretary, Office of Works, 11 March 1937, GAC File AA 3128/1 Part 1.
20. Letter from ambassador Sir Robert Craigie to Office of Works, 25 June 1938, GAC File AA 3128/1 Part 1.
21. This scheme is discussed by Adrian George in chapter 5.
22. Even before the war was over, some thought was being given to the future in this regard: 'After a heavy day, in the lighter parts of which I devoted myself to a memorandum on the

acquisition of English pictures and furniture for our Embassies and Government houses during the inevitable sales of private collections after the war…' John Colville, *op. cit.*, p. 540, entry for 10 March 1945.

23. C. Howard Smith, Foreign Office (writing as directed by the Foreign Secretary Sir John Simon) to Mrs. W. B. Woodrow, 29 May 1935, GAC File AA 634/1 Part 1.

24. See chapter 5.

25. Lord Salisbury to David Eccles, 15 August 1952, GAC File AA3054/2 Part 1. Works were sent out by Claude Rogers, Algernon Newton and Edward Seago, as well as a number of historic topographical prints of Australia.

26. Only the portraits of Lord Cromer and Lord Allenby were returned to the UK; they were later sent back to Cairo, where they are still on display.

27. Letter to Ministry of Works, 3 July 1952, GAC File AA 3010/1 Part 1.

28. '[I]n view of the insecurity of tenure of British Legations behind the Iron Curtain, it would be undesirable that really valuable or rare works of art should be sent to the official residences there.' Ambassador to Budapest to Anthony Eden, 10 July 1955, GAC File AA3004/1 Part 1; 'The atmosphere is heavy with coal smoke and tends to be damp as well', Norman Reddaway, ambassador to Poland, 13 October 1977, GAC File AA3076/1 Part 1.

29. Marcia Williams (Lady Falkender), *Inside No. 10* (London, 1972), p. 82.

30. 'Lowry's world is a world Harold Wilson understands, knowing it both from his father's recollections and from his own vivid childhood memories.' Marcia Williams (Lady Falkender), *Downing Street in Perspective* (London, 1983), p. 194; she described Lowry as Wilson's favourite artist.

31. The painting depicts a large abstract figure in red watching (or being watched by) three smaller abstract blue figures: the painting has also been known as *The Watchers* during its history.

32. This portrait was *not* hanging in the Cabinet Room at the time, as has been extensively and repeatedly misreported. The incident concerned a portrait of Gladstone (on loan from the National Portrait Gallery) that was hanging in Wilson's study (Bernard Donoughue, *Downing Street Diary: With Harold Wilson in No. 10* (London, 2005), pp. 656–657 (entry for 22 March 1976, as reported at the time to Donoughue by Wilson's Press Secretary Joe Haines).

33. Quoted in Peter Hennessy, *op. cit.*, p. 357.

34. Heath's changes to the picture displays at Number 10 are described in his autobiography *The Course of My Life* (London, 1998), pp. 459–461.

35. Dennis Skinner MP was particularly critical of Margaret Thatcher's 'Nicolae Ceaucescu school of art appreciation, as the Prime Minister disclosed that seventy state-owned paintings are currently adorning the walls of 10 Downing Street.' *The Independent*, 16 February 1990.

36. Nigel Lawson, *The View from No. 11: Memoirs of a Tory Radical* (London, 1992), p. 137.

37. This building had been annexed for use by 10 Downing Street in 2001.

38. As has been seen, the GAC has operated on a worldwide basis for over seventy years: some losses from its holdings over that time have been inevitable. These have now been reduced to a small trickle, but the British press continues to be obsessed by the subject, for example *The Daily Telegraph*, 1 November 2008 and *The Times*, 26 December 2008.

fig.47
Peter Tillemans
View of the Thames from Richmond Hill, c.1720–23
Oil on canvas

fig.48
Walter Richard Sickert
The Sisters Lloyd, 1888–89
Oil on canvas

fig.49
Henry Gales
The Derby Cabinet of 1867
Mezzotint, published c.1869

PEAS
ARE
THE NEW
BEANS

3. PEAS ARE THE NEW BEANS: TEN YEARS WITH THE GOVERNMENT ART COLLECTION

Richard Dorment

Towards the end of 1995 I received a telephone call from the director of the Government Art Collection (GAC). The purpose of her call was to sound me out: if asked, would I be willing to serve on the GAC's Advisory Committee on Works of Art? In those days I knew a great deal about Wendy Baron's work as a formidable art historian but nothing at all about her day job running the GAC. She had to explain that the Advisory Committee consisted of a chairman (the journalist and broadcaster John Tusa, who was then managing director of the Barbican) and the respective directors of the National Gallery, the Tate and the National Portrait Gallery. In addition, two people from the art world, including at least one art critic, served for a fixed term of three years, but the appointment could be renewed. The Advisory Committee met three times a year and Wendy assured me I'd find the discussions interesting.

'Interesting' turned out to be an understatement. In the ten years I was to be associated with the GAC it was the ideal vantage point from which to observe the profound shift in British attitudes towards the visual arts, which were nowhere more visible than in the workings of the Government Art Collection.

But all that was in the future. When I arrived at my first meeting in the GAC's offices in Soho in March 1996, sitting around a large table were Neil MacGregor (National Gallery), Nicholas Serota (Tate) and Charles Saumarez Smith (National Portrait Gallery). With such a distinguished group of voluntary advisors, it began to dawn on me that the Government took its art collection very seriously indeed. Present too was the critic, lecturer and collector Mary Rose Beaumont and two curators at the GAC whom I was to come to know and admire in the decade to come – Dr Mary Beal and Julia Toffolo.

Though the atmosphere was welcoming, Wendy Baron and John Tusa ran a tight ship. The meeting lasted two hours and in that time we got through a staggering amount of work. To be the director of a conventional gallery or museum is difficult enough, but my first thought as I listened to Wendy's opening report was that hers was an impossible job. Not only was the collection in her care scattered around the globe, but it was in constant flux. She had just returned from visits to the British diplomatic posts in Washington, Jakarta, Sydney, Melbourne and Paris. At each stop she met with the ambassador, high commissioner or consul-general, checked the safety and physical condition of the

fig.50
Bob and Roberta Smith
Peas Are the New Beans, 1999
Vinyl paint on panel

artworks owned by the GAC, and made sure each one was displayed and labelled appropriately.

When a minister takes up a new post, he or she is entitled to ask the GAC to change the art on the walls of their office to reflect their own tastes, politics and interests. Whenever this happened (and, of course, it is never *not* happening) someone from the GAC had to be on the spot to supervise the hanging of a painting or the installation of a statue. Art in our embassies isn't changed as often, but even if a picture remains permanently *in situ*, when it is removed for conservation or sent out on loan to an exhibition, the GAC attempts to find another picture of the right size and appropriate subject to replace it.

At the first meeting the topic under discussion was the commission for a monumental sculpture for the piazza outside the British high commission in Canberra. The director had already met with the Foreign and Commonwealth Office (FCO) to determine that the monument would serve as a focus for ceremonial and commemorative events

fig.51
Stephen Cox
Tribute Sculpture, 1996
Fouakir breccia sculpture with
bronze letters

rather than be, say, a war memorial. With that in mind, the committee had unanimously chosen Stephen Cox's proposal in consultation with the FCO and the high commissioner to Australia. In the months to come Cox would send maquettes of the carved stone monolith he'd designed for our approval (fig.51). This was not just a formality. Committee members did offer suggestions for improvements (Nicholas Serota, for example, was particularly concerned about how the sculptural mass sat on the base). During the course of the next year or so, we would monitor the progress of the commission from a distance, receiving photographs as the sculpture evolved and detailed reports when the stunning work was finally unveiled to enormous acclaim.

I also had my first taste of what I came to think of as topics-we-would-never-hear-the-end-of when the director raised the issue of publicising the work of the GAC by mounting an exhibition of selected works from the Collection at a venue in Great Britain. In the years to come we approached the Royal Academy and the Hayward Gallery but for one reason or another the project never got very far. It is only now, 15 years later, in the new and enlarged Whitechapel Gallery, that the exhibition is finally coming to fruition.

One reason the Advisory Committee was so keen to mount such an exhibition was in order to respond to misinformation about the GAC that appears constantly in the press. On any slow news day, I quickly discovered, a lazy journalist can manufacture a bit of cod outrage by asking why the British public is not allowed to see the art owned by the Government and paid for with taxpayers' money. No amount of explanation, we found, can persuade them that works of art which had been bought to be shown in Bangkok, Brasilia or Kuala Lampur would not be fulfilling their function if they remained in Great Britain for all to see.

And I would become familiar with the 'why-oh-why' stories asking why the Government buys works of art at all. The answer is that it does so for the same reason it maintains dignified embassies and government buildings: we are civilised people, and the presence in them of works of art of high quality signals the importance we place in this country on cultural and spiritual values. It isn't 'necessary' to have good art on the walls of government buildings – but most of us have seen foreign embassies where the sole decoration on otherwise bare walls is either a photo of the supreme leader or the national flag. For a relatively tiny annual expenditure, the GAC is there to tell the world who we are and what we are about.

That first meeting was now almost over. Before it was wound up, however, a ritual was enacted that was to become very familiar. Wendy Baron and John Tusa rose from their seats and invited us to follow them

YOUNG WOMAN

into an adjoining room that served as a sort of ad hoc gallery space. Here works of art that were either in transit or under consideration for purchase were displayed. It was time to look at the art the director had either already acquired from her modest discretionary fund (for which she did not need the committee's approval) or that she was considering for purchase.

As a general rule the committee would not recommend any work for purchase on the basis of photographs. If the picture or sculpture came from an art dealer it was brought into the GAC's offices. Only if the piece was to be sold at auction and could not be transported from Christie's or Sotheby's might we proceed on the basis of colour transparencies, but always with the proviso that each committee member would get down to the auction house in the following few days to look at the original and convey any misgivings by telephone to the director.

In the case of an historical work there might also be a short presentation by a GAC researcher. In every case, we were given a brief explanation of the painting's significance and the director's reasons for believing it would be a useful or important acquisition.

In the ten years I was on the Advisory Committee we considered for purchase artworks in every possible medium and of every possible subject and date. Many remain in my memory: superb prints by Gary Hume (fig.52) and Michael Craig-Martin, a pen-and-ink drawing by Michael Landy (see fig.103) and photos by Andy Goldsworthy, Darren Almond and Richard Billingham. I was particularly delighted with sculptures by Richard Deacon, Anish Kapoor and David Batchelor and paintings by John Hoyland, George Shaw and Fiona Rae (figs 53–56). There were only a handful of videos in the Collection, but the one that stands out for me is *Twenty Six (Drawing and Falling Things)*, which shows the minimalist performance artists John Wood and Paul Harrison pushing, jumping, sliding, falling and leaning against each other in a series of witty tableaux made with their own bodies (fig.57). I must add that we continued to collect historical paintings. Three of my favourites were Jacques-Laurent Agasse's *A Fishmonger's Shop*, Philippe Mercier's *The Young Artists*, and Frederic Leighton's *Mimbar of the Great Mosque at Damascus* (figs 58 and 59).

We had only a few rules to guide us. The GAC didn't buy anything that could possibly give offence (you'd be surprised how much contemporary art this knocks out) and we only bought works by artists who were either born in Britain or who lived here. A rare exception was Andy Warhol's silkscreen print of Queen Elizabeth II (fig. 93), but the reason for that is obvious.

fig.52
Gary Hume
Young Woman from the
Portraits series, 1998
Screenprint

87

fig.54
The entrance lobby to the
Cabinet Office, London with
Richard Deacon's ash and
aluminium sculpture
UW84DC#7, 2001

fig.55
David Batchelor
Shelf-like No. 5 (Green), 1999
Coloured acrylic sheets resting
on steel shelf

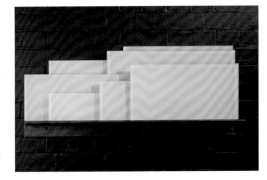

fig.57
John Wood and **Paul Harrison**'s
video installation *Twenty Six
(Drawing and Falling Things)*,
2000–01 installed at the
headquarters of the Council of
the European Union, Brussels,
during the UK's Presidency of
the European Union.

fig.53
Fiona Rae
Curl, 1997–98
Oil on canvas

fig.56
George Shaw
*Scenes from the Passion:
Valentine's Day*, 2004
Humbrol enamel paint on board

fig.58
Frederic, Lord Leighton
Mimbar of the Great Mosque at Damascus, 1873
Oil on canvas

The GAC tried hard to find the right pictures for the right locations. For example we placed Bridget Riley's important canvas *Reflection* (fig.60) in the Cairo embassy because the artist had begun the idea for this painting on a visit to Egypt using colours she'd seen in ancient wall paintings and tombs, but of course an added benefit is that an abstract painting is unlikely to offend the sensibility of a devout Muslim.

It was during these discussions that I felt the committee members were often most useful. None of us hesitated to say what we thought of a picture and why. It was very rare for us to approve for purchase every work of art brought in for our consideration – sometimes the piece just didn't arouse much enthusiasm, other times we felt the asking price was too high or that if we waited a better work by the same artist would come up at auction.

The director tries to get maximum value from the limited acquisition budget she is allocated every year by identifying young or emerging artists and acquiring their work while it is still affordable. This meant a never-ending round of visits to art galleries and artists' studios. After I'd been on the committee for a few years, I would often accompany Penny Johnson, Wendy's successor as director, on her visits to galleries, art fairs and studios. Usually Penny drew up the list of artists whose work she wished to see. But the GAC also had younger curators like Alistair Hudson, succeeded by Adrian George, who kept in touch with emerging

fig.59
Jacques-Laurent Agasse
A Fishmonger's Shop, 1840
Oil on canvas

fig.60
Bridget Riley
Reflection, 1982
Oil on linen

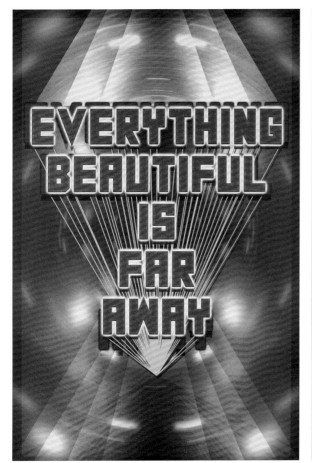

fig.61
Mark Titchner
Everything Beautiful is Far Away,
2003–05
Unique archival inkjet print on
aluminium and acrylic sheet

fig.62
Mark Titchner
Only the First Step is Difficult, 2005
Unique archival inkjet print on
aluminium and acrylic sheet

artists, and the director's studio and gallery visits were sometimes made in response to a recommendation by them.

That's how we came to visit the studio of Mark Titchner (figs 61 and 62) – an artist whose work I did not know – and subsequently to purchase not one but two important early pieces. All this happened several years before he was nominated for the Turner Prize. For an art critic on a daily broadsheet, it can be hard to keep up with new trends and emerging artists. While I was on the Advisory Committee I was able to see a much broader range and variety of new art than I do now – simply because the GAC curators steered me down paths I'd never have found on my own.

Here I must add that, as advisors, we only offered opinions. The director had the final say. However, I have always considered myself personally responsible for the GAC's purchase of a work by that extraordinary artist Bob and Roberta Smith. Penny and I were at an art fair when I spotted a little painting on board by him that simply read in multi-coloured lettering: 'PEAS ARE THE NEW BEANS' (fig.50).

Yes, it was dead silly, but it didn't cost much and it wasn't easy to find a work by Bob and Roberta that could be displayed in a public building without causing offence. Secretly, I wondered whether anyone would ever want to show it. I later learned that the work has proved enormously popular and is always out on display, so far in the offices of the bean counters at the Treasury and the Cabinet Office.

fig.63
Roger Hiorns
Nunhead, 2004
Engines, steel, aluminium, plastics, rubber, copper sulphate
Courtesy Arts Council England

At other times outstanding works of art might be rejected for unusual reasons. At a preview of the second Frieze Art Fair Penny reserved a piece by future Turner Prize nominee Roger Hiorns – a BMW engine the artist had covered in copper sulphate. By the time she saw it, blue crystals had grown over its surface, transforming the utilitarian motor into an object of exotic beauty laced with a whiff of danger. While copper sulphate is poisonous, it was conservation concerns that prevented us from buying it. Even if it had been placed under a Perspex covering, it would still have posed too great a challenge to conservators (fig.63).

The GAC's acquisitions policy is slightly different from that of other museums or art galleries. On occasion the director will purchase a work of limited aesthetic distinction for its links with a particular country or even a particular building, such as *View of the Tagus and the Tower of Belém from the British Legation*, Lisbon, a watercolour by George Lennard Lewis, purchased in 2000. While I was on the committee an example of a painting that was both ravishing as well as being historically apposite for a particular building was George Hayter's portrait of the daughters of Lord Stuart de Rothsay, British ambassador

to Paris in the early 19th century (fig.64). As a work of art it would have looked lovely wherever it was hung. But the subject made it ideal for the embassy in Paris.

In April 1997 the incomparable Wendy Baron retired after 19 years as director. Though I'm sure she'd have loved every minute of what was about to happen, she never saw at first hand the change in the GAC that occurred after the Labour party won the general election a month later. Overnight, it seemed, the demand for modern art outstripped the GAC's ability to supply it. Though we didn't realise it at the time, what we were witnessing was a complete reversal of taste and fashion in Britain. Within a few months of taking up her new job, Penny Johnson and her team faced the daunting task of allocating works of art for the offices of over 60 new ministers, not to mention personally dealing with the Foreign Secretary and Chancellor of the Exchequer. For the first time in 30 years, historical works in Numbers 10 and 11 Downing Street were removed and replaced by modern paintings, photos and sculptures.

Most Labour ministers wanted contemporary or modern art – which may have had something to do with Labour's wish to brand itself as modern, but also reflected a new-found national enthusiasm for contemporary art that had been set in motion in the 1990s by publicity given to the Turner Prize and the exhibitions staged by Charles Saatchi.

The GAC's was always a working collection, but never had it worked so hard. For example, soon after Penny Johnson's arrival the new ambassador in Paris asked her to introduce more contemporary British art in the residence, and she therefore inaugurated the lively series of changing displays in the conservatory-like Glazed Galleries. Unusually, these mini surveys of new British art were changed with every new ambassador and continue to this day.

Some pieces shown at the ambassador's residence in Paris are instantly recognisable (well, to most Brits) – Rachel Whiteread's resin model for the sculpture on the fourth plinth in Trafalgar Square (fig.65), Gillian Wearing's iconic video *Dancing in Peckham* (fig.114) and Simon Patterson's reconfiguration of the map of the London Underground into a kind of cultural history of the world (*The Great Bear*, fig.66) all come to mind. Darren Almond's moonlit photographs of Flatford Mill (fig.67) – the building made famous in Constable's painting – are not so well known, but like all the artworks I've just mentioned it could only have been created by a British artist. At a time when a lot of the work shown in Parisian galleries could be described as 'Euroart', such quirky, distinctive shows were surely influential in shaping French perception of the renaissance in the visual arts that was then taking place across the Channel.

fig.64
George Hayter
The Hon. Charlotte Stuart (1817–1861) and the Hon. Louisa Stuart (1818–1891), Daughters of Sir Charles Stuart, Baron Stuart de Rothesay (1779–1845) Diplomat, 1830
Oil on canvas

fig.65
Rachel Whiteread
Untitled (Trafalgar Square Plinth), 1999
Plaster and resin

The Great Bear

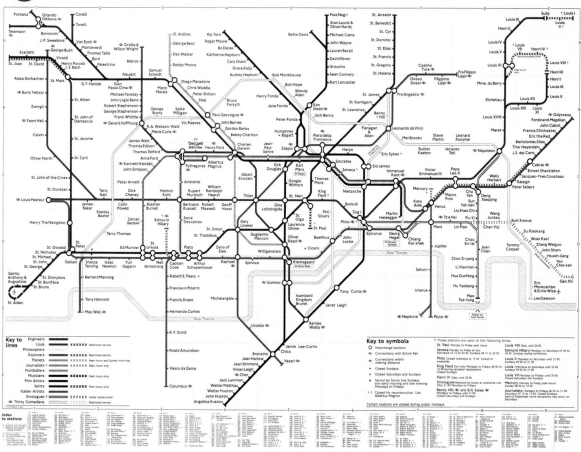

fig.66
Simon Patterson
The Great Bear, 1992
Colour lithograph

Because the new Minister for the Arts, Mark Fisher, had worked in the arts he was quick to appreciate the role the GAC could play in the new government's ambitious building programme. He understood, too, that with increased demand for modern and contemporary art but no increase in our annual purchase grant, new ways would have to be found to bring the best contemporary art into the Collection.

There was only one place to look for additional support – the Foreign and Commonwealth Office. Until then, most new government buildings foraged for furnishings and decoration after the builders had left. Art was an afterthought. Now Penny Johnson asked the then Overseas Estate Department (the department within the Foreign Office responsible for building and maintaining foreign embassies) always to consult with the GAC before commissioning new work. Not only did they agree, but they asked us to purchase much of the art that would be shown in the new buildings. This was an important change in the role of the GAC, for now we would become involved at an early stage of the design process. Art would become an integral part of each new government building, not a later add-on. What's more, the GAC got the Government to agree that the GAC should oversee the installation and maintenance of any work that it purchased or commissioned.

It is fair to say that the new government wanted to use art to give major foreign embassies a makeover – or at least a new image. But it was impossible for us to realise the Government's good intentions on our limited budget. Since we had the expertise but not the money, and the FCO had a budget for commissioning art for new buildings but no

fig.67
Darren Almond
Flatford @ Fullmoon, 2000
Lamda print

fig.68
The British embassy, Moscow

curatorial expertise, it made sense that the two government departments should work together to make sure that what money was available was spent wisely. On an entirely practical level this joining of forces eliminated the possibility that a building's architect might act unilaterally to purchase an artwork that looked attractive in the gallery but proved a nightmare to install and difficult to maintain.

Within six months of Penny Johnson's arrival the committee learned that she and her team had been asked to work with the architects of two of the embassies then under construction. The first was Michael Wilford's in Berlin, and the second was Ahrends, Burton and Koralek's in Moscow (fig.68). Penny visited the still unfinished buildings, then she invited the architects to show plans, elevations and scale models to the Advisory Committee. Ideas were solicited from us all and we were consulted both when buying works of art and at every stage in the commissioning process.

Let me take the case of the Moscow embassy, which was opened by the Princess Royal on 17 May 2000, as a perfect example of how the GAC worked. The ultra-modern building was a light, glass-fronted structure comprising government offices, conference rooms, an area for issuing visas and a medical centre – as well as flats, tennis courts, a gym and swimming pool for British diplomats and their families. It didn't replace the old embassy – an historic building opposite the Kremlin – which remained in use as the ambassador's residence (and has since been refurbished). Since the new building was designed in the

1990s it was only appropriate that the overwhelming number of artworks in it should be made by artists who emerged in that decade.

In the long dark Russian winter, it would be hard to imagine a more exuberant welcome to the embassy than *Lighthouse* (fig.69) the mural-sized canvas by Michael Craig-Martin that dominates the entrance hall. The bold still life consists of simple outline drawings of a giant torch surrounded by an open book, a globe, a chair and a filing cabinet – all rendered in a riot of intense, saturated colours ranging from turquoise and yellow to sky-blue and apple green. Only the monumental torch that dominates the composition is white – its size, shape and lack of colour 'rhyming' with the actual three-dimensional columns in the main hall. Ordinary as the objects shown in it are, each was chosen for its symbolic value – the torch proclaims that Britain is a beacon of light to the world. Behind it, the globe refers to international diplomacy, the book symbolises learning, and the filing cabinet the mundane activities

fig.69
The interior of the British embassy, Moscow showing **Michael Craig-Martin**'s painting *Lighthouse*, 1999

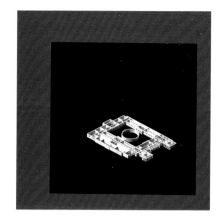

fig.70
Langlands and Bell
*Space / Object (Pushkin
State Museum of Fine Arts,
Moscow – The British Museum,
London)*, 1999
Diptych framed and glazed
sculptural panels: wood, paint,
lacquer, glass

that go on in an embassy. Since the canvas rises 20 feet almost to touch the ceiling, it so dominates the entrance foyer that it is impossible for me to imagine what the embassy would look like without it.

Elsewhere in the building hang two shallow boxes by Ben Langlands and Nikki Bell (fig.70), each containing a three dimensional isometric scale model of a building. From a distance, all the viewer sees is a dense maze of lines, but step close enough to read the label and you realise that one shows the plan of the Pushkin Museum in Moscow and the other its equivalent in London, the British Museum. Both buildings date from the early 19th century and both display works of art. What the artists subtly suggest is that buildings, like countries, may look strange from far away, but as you come closer the distortions created by distance disappear and they begin to resemble those we are familiar with back home. My favourite example of how sensitively these artists used works of art to suggest shared cultural links between this country and Russia was the young British artist Juan Cruz's remarkable series of works based on stage directions by Chekhov. To understand it, you must read the explanatory label, which explains that Chekhov wrote elaborate directions to all his plays, minutely describing in words the imaginary scene he intended his audiences to see when the curtain rose. In them he specified the kind of furniture that should be used in each scene, where he wanted it placed, where the actors should stand and what they should be wearing and any sound effects that we should be hearing. In practice, this means that all productions of *The Cherry Orchard* or *The Seagull* look essentially alike, because Chekhov gave future production designers very little leeway to interpret his plays.

fig.71
The artist **Juan Cruz** installing
his works at the British embassy,
Moscow.

This is the reason that the first scene in the second act of *Uncle Vanya* looks broadly the same whether it is performed in Moscow, London, Paris or Berlin. In other words, we all carry around within us a mental vision of Chekhov's world. What Cruz did was to translate Chekhov's stage directions for scenes in *Tatyana Repin*, *The Seagull* and *The*

Wedding, then lightly stencil each short passage on the embassy walls in pencil (fig.71).

The faintness of the lettering encourages the passer-by to stop, to look closer and to read carefully – and in reading to discover that the mental picture we have of the scene described is every bit as vivid as a painted picture would be. Seen in the British embassy in Moscow, the work took on extraordinary resonance, reminding anyone who saw it that, although Chekhov writes so specifically about Russia, his plays transcend nationality. An English person pictures each character and each scene in exactly the same way as a Russian does. In a way that is certainly not true of Shakespeare (where the same play can be set in, say, contemporary London or Berlin in the 1930s), Chekhov's art is universal.

What came to fascinate me was how different each of the GAC's interventions in these new buildings turned out to be. The size of the atrium in the new Berlin embassy provided the GAC with an ideal opportunity to fill one of the glaring gaps in the Collection by acquiring an important sculpture by Tony Cragg, who, in addition to being one of this country's best-known artists, also lives and works in Germany. That's how the GAC came to commission his remarkable *Dancing Columns*, two monumental towers made of stacked layers of local sandstone (fig.72). Cragg's work introduces a powerful element of dynamic destabilisation into the serene atrium of Michael Wilford's classically inspired building. A prominent feature in the design was a monumental staircase with recessed niches which Wilford originally intended to fill with statues. The problem was that it would be impossible to find, let alone afford, antique or neoclassical marbles of the right scale. And

fig.72
The artist **Tony Cragg** supervising the installation of his sculptures at the British embassy, Berlin, 2000

101

even if it had been possible, we worried that the sheer scale of Cragg's massive sculpture would overwhelm conventional statuary. The solution was radical: a wall drawing by distinguished British artist David Tremlett, who produced a dramatic and highly coloured abstract design that held its own beside the Cragg without competing with it (fig.73). Purists, I'm sure, would have preferred to leave the walls white and the niches empty, but for me the result was a stunning success, lending warmth and colour and visual excitement to the cavernous atrium.

In October 1999 the GAC moved from Soho to new premises off Tottenham Court Road. One of our first discussions revolved around a fascinating question of conservation. The director reported that an outdoor wooden sculpture by David Nash in the grounds of the Tokyo embassy was unfortunately riddled with termites and no longer suitable for display. Left alone, the piece would cease to exist in a few years. To make a decision on how best to treat the problem, we had to bring the piece back to this country. But before we could bring it back for conservation, it needed to be fumigated – and the cost of fumigation proved to be exorbitant. The alternative was to destroy the work *in situ* and replace it with another piece by the same artist. Though I'm compressing discussions that in reality took place over a period of more than a year, in the end we sought advice from the artist himself and decided the piece should be destroyed.

By the turn of the century we were discussing the role the GAC might play in any future renovation of the interior of 10 Downing Street. Of course the GAC has always provided pictures, both historical and modern, for its public and private rooms. But we only added window dressing to what was, in truth, a building that desperately needed the expertise of architectural historians before undergoing a complete decorative refurbishment. Only then would it be restored to something that resembled what it had once been. Decades of indifference had left a hodgepodge of rooms with no atmosphere, and little evidence of the house's rich history. The Blairs encouraged group visits to the house but I often wondered what school children and church groups made of it all (fig.74).

Though we were regularly over at Number 10 hanging new pictures and taking others away, there was not much the GAC could do on its own about the fabric or decoration of the building. In the end we had to admit to ourselves that unless private donors stepped forward to restore the house in the same way Americans had restored the White House, no government would dare be seen dealing with the problem, knowing the tabloid headlines about wasteful spending that were certain to follow. All this happened years before the MPs' expenses scandal, so now I don't expect to see any improvement during my lifetime.

fig.73
Tony Cragg
Dancing Columns, 2000
Sandstone
with **David Tremlett**'s *Wall Drawing*, 2000, in the background at the British embassy, Berlin, 2000

103

fig.74
On the eve of the Ashes series in Australia, former British Prime Minister Tony Blair, plays cricket with children from the East Kent Cricket club inside Number 10 Downing Street on 22 November 2006.

Of course we had our failures and frustrations too. One of the most irritating occurred when we were buying works for the Moscow embassy. The GAC did not have an important piece by the artists Gilbert and George, whose imagery is difficult in much the same way as Francis Bacon's can be – violent, expressionistic and often deliberately offensive in terms of the words and images used in the design. But their art was particularly suitable for Moscow since they had staged a triumphantly successful exhibition there in the early 1990s and so were familiar names to gallery-going Russians. Penny found at the dealer Anthony d'Offay a pair of photo collages which were not just exhibitable but had strong visual links with Russian Constructivist design of the 1920s. Anthony d'Offay consulted Gilbert and George on the sale, because they will not sell their work to banks or corporate collections. Before agreeing to sell to the GAC, the artists asked to see where their works would be displayed, both because their photo-based art must not be exposed to sunlight and also because they don't believe art should be used as decoration in bland public spaces. When we showed them that the works would be seen in an interior part of the building and in a prominent position they agreed to the sale, so we felt we'd been lucky. The purchase was about to be made when, incredibly, a diary piece appeared in *The Times*, reporting that the ambassador in Moscow, Sir Andrew Wood, was not keen on the two works by Gilbert and George. Once these words were in print, whether true or not, that was that. The sale was killed and to this day the British government owns nothing of real significance by the most important British artists to emerge in the 1960s and 1970s.

The GAC does everything in its power to ensure that ambassadors understand their obligation to look after the works of art in their embassies. Before all new ambassadors take up their posts, they visit the GAC for a briefing. GAC staff also give a standard talk to ambassadors' spouses and management officers in which they emphasise the importance of notifying the GAC about any changes to the works of art. The ambassador and the staff are given a copy of the GAC's 'Conditions of Loan', stipulating that ambassadors must consult the GAC before taking the initiative in the acquisition of a new work or when placing any work on embassy grounds. Also included are instructions for their care, and measures to take in case of emergency or disaster. From 1980 onward, the GAC has provided information folders to the embassy personnel giving some interpretative material about the works. In the late 1990s, this was updated to include an image of every work of art on loan to the embassy.

These measures were intended to prevent second-rate or kitsch work being shown in government buildings – and also so that the GAC could be aware of any potential problems regarding a work's conservation and general maintenance. After all, the reason museum directors like Serota, Saumarez Smith and MacGregor gave so freely of their time and expertise was to ensure that our government offices and foreign embassies weren't filled with tat. Nothing is more worrying to us than a rogue ambassador and it can be frustrating when an ambassador decides unilaterally to acquire a work for the embassy, even if he finds private funding for it. On the one or two occasions when this happened, we had to tell the ambassador that in our judgment it did not reflect the best in British art.

This applied to the display of art as well as its purchase. Having seen photographs of how paintings had been hung at one important embassy, it became clear that it was necessary for a member of the GAC staff to be present to oversee the installation when any new work was sent there on loan.

Politicians weren't nearly as difficult as ambassadors. I remember only one instance in which a politician attempted to interfere in the way the GAC worked, and come to think of it, he was put up to it by a former ambassador. In his new capacity as chief executive of British Trade International, a former ambassador visited Leeds in the company of a Minister for Trade. On that visit the ambassador saw a work he liked the look of. The minister duly wrote to the committee drawing it to our attention.

Unfortunately the committee thought the piece second rate and refused to buy it. When the minister then summoned the director to his office for an explanation, I agreed to accompany her. The meeting began with the minister demanding to know why the GAC rarely bought works from art dealers outside of London and – come to that – why most of the committee members were based in London. In answer to the first question Penny Johnson explained that the GAC inevitably buys from London dealers since, wherever they live in Great Britain, the artists themselves want to be shown in London galleries. The GAC owned a great number of works by artists living outside London, but usually they had been purchased in the capital.

It was also inevitable that the Committee should reflect a bias towards London – since the Tate, the National Gallery and the National Portrait Gallery were all here, not in Swanage. Then too, London has a vibrant art scene with most young artists choosing to pursue their careers here. One good thing came of this meeting, which was that in the years to come we made a conscious effort to recruit curators, critics or gallery directors from outside London to sit on the Advisory Committee. Of the many anecdotes about the GAC I could tell here, the one I cherish most had its origins in October 1998 when the Home Secretary asked whether there was any scope for the GAC to support the Koestler Awards. This is an excellent scheme to encourage the creative endeavours of young offenders, prisoners and patients in special hospitals. For all the sympathy we had for the project, we had to reply that our acquisition policy was based on the intrinsic interest and importance of each work. However worthy the motive, the GAC could not buy art of questionable aesthetic merit in order to further the Government's social policy.

Six years later, in 2004, the GAC was commissioning work for the new Home Office on Marsham Street (fig.75). By now the excellent Julia Somerville had managed the impossible by replacing the irreplaceable John Tusa as our chairman. As we opened the initial discussions, the GAC suggested that we ask Turner Prize winner Jeremy Deller and Alan Kane – well known for making art by forming collections of objects that reveal something profound about the cultural identity of this country – to make an installation out of works of art chosen from the Koestler Awards, a very different project from the straightforward acquisition of prisoner art as had been proposed some years earlier. Deller and Kane grouped dozens of these works together (as opposed to scattering individual pictures throughout the building) to create a fascinating work of art that was 'about' the creative endeavours being done in prisons, the wealth of talent lost to crime and drugs, and the Government's concern for the rehabilitation of prisoners. *The Home Office Collection of Art from Prisons* could have had no greater impact than in its new home, the Home Office.

The Home Office was the last big project I was involved in before leaving the GAC in 2005. Here, it was a great advantage that at the

fig.75
The façade of the Home Office,
London, showing architectural
enhancements by the artist
Liam Gillick

figs 76 and 77
Georgie Hopton's project – titled
Keep the Home Fires Burning –
being installed at the Home Office,
London shortly before opening
in 2000

suggestion of the GAC the artist Liam Gillick had already been commissioned to enliven the exterior of the building with a multicoloured glass canopy. In his quasi-curatorial role Liam initially provided us with a list of contemporary artists whose work he hoped to see in the vast interior, and with that Penny Johnson and Alastair Hudson (and later Adrian George) met with the sculptors Eva Rothschild, Gary Webb, Roger Hiorns, Simon Periton, Georgie Hopton (figs 76 and 77), Emma Kay and Runa Islam – as well as with Toby Paterson.

There were hiccups – Simon Periton originally proposed creating a sculpture in the form of a band of barbed wire in pink neon, but it was

fig.78
The artist **Simon Periton** (with Georgie Hopton) inspecting his sculpture *Charm Bracelet*, 2000 at the Home Office, London

fig.79
Gary Webb
Untitled 2005
Mixed media, rotating sculptural
project at the Home Office, London

felt that the joke didn't work in that particular location, so he changed the 'wire' to chain link (fig.78). But the one piece that we expected might cause difficulty was Gary Webb's monumental, neo-Pop ice lolly in psychedelic colours that moved slowly round on its rotating base (fig.79). Quiet good taste it was not. But to my surprise, Fiona MacTaggart, the minister responsible for signing off our work at the Home Office, seemed to love it and I have to say that of all the many artworks the GAC either commissioned or bought during my time there, it is the one that to this day gives me the most pleasure. If 'peas are the new beans', then during my time on the Advisory Committee art became the new rock 'n' roll. It was my privilege to help the GAC show the world that this country fully appreciates art's power to entertain, delight, empower and enlighten.

fig.80
Chantal Joffe
Red-haired Woman in the Park, 2003
Oil on board

fig.81
James Joseph Jacques Tissot
On the River, 1871
Oil on canvas

fig.82
Daniel Maclise
*The Chivalric Vow of the Ladies
of the Peacock*, 1835
Oil on canvas

fig.83
Hew Locke
Serpent of the Nile (Sejant), 2007
C-type photograph mounted
on aluminium

4. THINGS: A CONVERSATION BETWEEN CORNELIA PARKER, ANDREW RENTON AND PENNY JOHNSON

fig.85
R. B. Kitaj
The Jewish Question from the portfolio *In Our Time: Covers for a Small Library After the Life for the Most Part*, 1970
Screenprint

fig.86
Anya Gallaccio
Broken English August '91 from the portfolio *Screen*, 1997
Screenprint

fig.84
Thomas Phillips
George Gordon Noel Byron, 6th Baron (1788–1824), Poet, 1814
Oil on canvas

On Wednesday 29 September 2010, Andrew Renton, a member of the GAC's Advisory Committee, interviewed the artist Cornelia Parker who had been exploring the Collection to select works for an exhibition at the Whitechapel Gallery in 2011. Penny Johnson was present too.

AR: You've been rummaging round the Collection for a few months. I guess it's impossible to get a full picture of what the Collection is, but what have you found that has surprised you about it – what has it taught you?

CP: I became very aware looking at the Collection that its content has been determined by being on show in very particular environments. That it can't risk being too overtly political or inflammatory. There are certain things I noticed in my research that I wondered if they had ever been borrowed, that seemed to be there because they had been part of a larger portfolio. For example R. B. Kitaj's series of book covers – there's one of a book called *The Jewish Question* (fig.85) that I can't imagine being displayed on a wall anywhere. Or something like Anya Gallaccio's *Broken English August '91* (fig.86), which has such a great

title, one that has all kinds of connotations. I'm interested in their exhibition history. I was trying to look for those spiky kinds of works, just because there's such a lot of beautiful landscapes, paintings of royalty and works by the Bloomsbury Group in the Collection – things that wouldn't be provocative in any way when shown in a government context. Except for satirical cartoons, it is only in the last 30 years you can see things emerging that are more politically ambiguous in the more contemporary work.

AR: I would imagine that if we kept looking at things politically we'd be able to read everything in the Collection in that way. The question is: what does it avoid? What does each work avoid in terms of contentiousness and what does it embrace? Are there cartoons, for example, because they are constructed to be a permitted form of critique, within the social order of things? On the other hand you raise an interesting question that begs the much bigger question about the selection criteria; you mention works and tendencies that didn't get into the Collection. But what's also interesting is what has been inherited, i.e. what entered the Collection in its early years, given that this is a collection that has been actively acquiring works for more than a century. What you have then is a lot of forgetting. The thing that isn't forgotten, funnily enough, is the artwork, but what is forgotten is the reason why the artwork is chosen then. I think that's the really interesting part.

CP: I think that's what I became aware of when I was looking at this collection. Unlike the Tate's, this one feels like it's an extension of our diplomatic service, which has shaped the criteria for choosing, especially with regard to, say, multiples of things. There's a particular pair of paintings I was thinking of – George V and his consort Princess Mary of Teck (figs 87 and 88) – which I think there are around 20 copies of. These are huge paintings, perfect, I'm sure, for embassies all over the world.

AR: But it does beg the question… why 20 copies of a painting?

PJ: Earlier in the 20th century, copies of royal portraits were sent to almost every overseas government building where they served a clear diplomatic purpose. Most of them have gradually been added to the GAC's inventory.

CP: What I love about trying to curate some of this work is there are so many backstories to all these images. Their provenances are fascinating; it's wonderful to see where they've been and where they now reside.

AR: I think that's one of the things that may be unique about this collection. First of all, we know that it's an incredibly well-used collection; it's a collection where the vast majority of it is out… and it's out there.

fig.87
Sir Samuel Luke Fildes (after)
King George V (1865–1936),
Reigned 1910–36, date unknown
Oil on canvas

fig.88
William Llewellyn (after)
Mary of Teck (1867–1953),
Queen Consort of King George V,
date unknown
Oil on canvas

And sometimes – and I think this may be where your interest lies – works go out like Kurtz in [Joseph Conrad's] *Heart of Darkness*, and they go a bit native. After about two decades they come back and they're not quite what they were. I'm not talking in terms of condition, but in terms of the kind of meaning that…

CP: … that they've accrued?

AR: … accrued to the work of art as it's been on a journey, and I think that's one of the things that seems to characterise the Government Art Collection. Because of the 'officialness' of the works moving around the world they, by definition, have stories that accrue to them. They have their own narratives and they make their own journeys. For a curator, or for anyone who's interested in art, I think that's extremely interesting. So your starting point, about the things that you can't do, makes this collection extremely interesting. The works that do make the grade, that can travel and participate in the Collection's role, tell a story through the journeys they make.

CP: I'm interested to see whether things ended up in a corridor in an embassy or in the more intimate quarters of a leading politician. Whether they are exhibited in a public or private space as well. Some of these things would be in private accommodation as well wouldn't they?

PJ: Official residences. So, they're not private and…

CP: … because they're always entertaining in them.

PJ: Yes, works in official residences are placed in representational areas, i.e. the public spaces used for events or entertaining, not in their private quarters, if indeed they have private quarters. And in the case of the Prime Minister, the Foreign Secretary and the Chancellor – who all have official residences – that means in their public spaces.

CP: So they're not allowed to have them in the bedrooms? *[Laughs.]*

AR: This leads to an interesting question in terms of 'choosing'. We're trying to understand some of the decisions that get made, and we're trying to understand how things go half way round the world and come back again. And it seems to me that the Collection bears witness to several types of choice. There's that conventional choice when a work of art goes into a collection – that work is selected and it's bought. Today it's done through committee, and there's a rigorous process of research and ratification, sitting round a board table making well-researched decisions. But there's a second kind of choice that I'm really interested in, namely the quirky ones that are made by the people who are entitled to borrow works from the Collection. Of course, we might assume that since a lot of these works end up in embassies and in politicians' offices that they're probably going to be very conventional, very predictable safe choices. But I think there must also be some eccentric choices, where the person chooses to represent themselves through the works that are on their wall. I'm sure that that is something you might dig up as you start to see some of these works.

PJ: We do make a pre-selection with some of the politicians and ambassadors because we know the space, but there are times when they just come and look at works and go through the racks.

CP: Yes, I presume politicians have very little time really for doing lots of in-depth research. So with a text work like *Peas are the New Beans* (fig.50) there must be certain politicians you wouldn't present that to…

PJ: Exactly.

AR: *Peas are the New Beans*! If one situates that as a work in a long and noble history of British art, it's an absolute manifestation of Britishness. That's the other thing that we're all very shy to talk about; that it's a British collection, of British art, give or take the Warhol portrait of the Queen. It's absolutely about British creativity.

CP: Context can be all. A work that's not overtly political can become so in certain environments… I know from showing my own work that something seemingly benign on home turf can be read very differently when shown in another country. I made a piece called *The Edge of England* (fig.89) which consisted of a suspended wall of chalk from Beachy Head, which when it was shown in a biennale in Australia was seen as a post-colonial statement. Another of my suspended pieces, *Neither From Nor Towards*, was created from beachcombed bricks that had come from a house that fell off the White Cliffs of Dover and had been turned into pebbles by the sea. I made it originally to show in Germany, so it literally fell off the White Cliffs of Dover and landed in Leipzig. That same piece was shown in Slovenia in a museum in Ljubljana, when the Sarajevo war was on. There were a lot of refugees there and they said, well for us this is a very political piece and is reflecting what's going on in our country. Context can make you read works very differently. Government offices, Number 10, various embassies all over the world are flagship places to show British culture – this is a great proving ground. It means the works can become more elastic in their meaning.

AR: So the meaning of a work seems to change in relation to the history…

CP: Its viewing history?

AR: Its viewing history, or its selection history, or… because it's a public collection, inevitably there are works in the collection that are often signature works. Often, of course, they're so signature that by definition they're not around for us to see, because they've been sent away. We

fig.89
Cornelia Parker
The Edge of England, 1999

121

fig.90
Paul Nash
Event on the Downs, 1934
Oil on canvas

were just talking about the Paul Nash – *Event on the Downs* (fig.90) – it is a perfect example in that it's such a key work for the Collection, and a measure of the success of the work is that it rarely comes home.

PJ: Although in fact it does as it's often recalled for public exhibitions.

AR: So it's constantly bouncing backwards and forwards?

PJ: Yes, in the last few years the exhibition history of that painting is quite extraordinary…

AR: So what's the most used work? Can one quantify that?

PJ: It's difficult. Some of the more generic works might move around London from ministerial office to ministerial office but works bought for a specific location – such as the portrait of Lord Byron in Athens by Thomas Phillips (fig.84) – move far less, unless they're requested for loan.

AR: So they're used in many contexts… There might be a work that sits in the same place for 20 years, but also there are works that have been to more locations than any other…

PJ: We have a Daniel Egerton landscape of Mexico (fig.36), which was presented in 1936, and went straight out to Mexico. It's been on exhibition in the USA and Mexico, but it hasn't been back to the UK so we're quite keen to get it back for the GAC exhibition at the Whitechapel Gallery.

AR: So your conservation department will be sort of waiting at the door, like in an episode of *ER*, to bring it in for emergency treatment…

PJ: A conservator has examined the painting and there have been a couple of visits to Mexico in the last 10 years, so we have seen the work; we just haven't ever had it back here. So those are ones that don't move – another would be the portrait in Paris of the sculptor Antonio Canova by George Hayter (fig.91). That has a very specific history that ties it to the embassy so that's why it stays where it is.

fig.91
George Hayter
*Antonio Canova (1757–1822)
Italian sculptor*, 1817
Oil on canvas

fig.92
David Dawson
Lucian Freud painting the Queen,
2001
C-type photograph

fig.93
Andy Warhol
Queen Elizabeth II of the
United Kingdom from the portfolio
Reigning Queens (Royal Edition),
1985
Screenprint with diamond dust
on board

CP: So are things bought for very specific locations?

PJ: We do buy things for very specific locations. I've just installed a display in Los Angeles and we commissioned Donald Urquhart to do one of his *A to Z* black ink drawings (fig.38). And we bought a Kathy Prendergast map of North West America which has everything blacked out except for the towns or settlements represented by a white dot. In the top right-hand corner, there are parallel trails of little dots that indicate people coming in their wagons from east to west. It's extraordinary…

CP: So it maps out all those pioneering routes.

PJ: Yes, and it was bought specifically for the consulate-general in Los Angeles.

CP: I love the various images of the Queen in the Collection – Andy Warhol's younger Queen versus the photograph of Lucian Freud painting the older one (figs 92 and 93).

AR: But isn't it interesting that the Warhol portrait of the Queen is in a way more reflective of the way that the Queen might have been represented, or any royalty might have been represented in the Collection historically, whereas today it takes Warhol to copy that, so he needs the official image, if you like, to…

CP: It's like the Chinese whisper of the Queen.

124

AR: Correct. But I think something else has happened in this collection over the past couple of decades that has changed not just the way that, by definition, it's contemporary, but also how the work of art itself will function in a different way. When we look at 'official' painting – painting that is a reflection of the authority structures of the British Empire, the King, the Queen – today there's less desire for those to form part of any kind of hang, or any kind of installation. I can't put my finger on it exactly, but I'm tempted to say there's a more self-deprecating kind of choice that's made by the people who are both acquiring the work and selecting the work for display. So you end up with a work like Martin Creed's *Work No. 253: THINGS* (fig.94) which is just…

CP: Great!

AR: I think it's an extraordinarily important work of British art. But it's important because it doesn't claim a universal authority for itself. And so it's a reflection of British self-deprecation. There's a kind of modesty of intention in the work that I think is marking the newer generation of artists whose work is entering the Government Art Collection. And also what we want from our art.

CP: Going back to the photograph [by David Dawson] of the Queen being painted by Lucian Freud. I don't think the Queen really liked the finished portrait did she? She much preferred having Rolf Harris paint her, and we all know the story of that through the media. So it's quite wonderful to see Lucian Freud in the act of painting this portrait – with the Queen sitting uncomfortably there. It tells a more ambiguous story. We're allowed to show things that are a little bit more self-reflective and self-deprecating now.

fig.94
Martin Creed
Work No. 253: THINGS, 2000
Neon

fig.95
Damien Hirst
Pardaxin, 2004
Household gloss paint on canvas

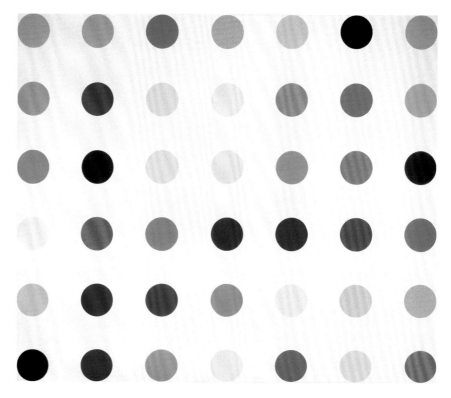

PJ: I think there has been a shift in perception. I arrived in 1997, three weeks before the General Election and I have seen a shift in what's more acceptable.

CP: There's more transparency – you can show your vulnerabilities, which was much harder when Britain had an empire.

AR: I think what Penny's just signalled is that if historically the art was a reflection of what you want your social order to be, actually the Collection now looks to the art to interpret the way that our world is today. And of course that's the way it should be. It's very much a sign of the times, that the art actually has a proactive function. I don't think it's an accident that in the past decade we've seen the very things that define a new type of Britishness coming though the art, whether it's a Damien Hirst spot painting (fig.95), or whatever…

CP: I think of a Jeremy Deller or David Shrigley (figs 96 and 97) or Martin Parr, who say provocative things with humour.

PJ: Grayson Perry's work?

CP: Yes, Grayson Perry's another one.

PJ: Perry's *Print for a Politician* (fig.98) is on the Chancellor of the Exchequer's – George Osborne's – wall now.

CP: I do love that print. Somehow the idiosyncratic British observational humour becomes much more edgy in that environment… Some of these slight works by Martin Parr or Shrigley can punch way above their weight.

AR: Can I shift the subject a little bit and ask you whether with a collection such as this – one that is clearly not thematically constructed – you can see any themes that emerge from it? I wonder if there are any things that just keep coming back? There may even be truisms about any collection, but particularly so about this one. I mean, do we keep seeing landscapes, for example?

CP: There are lots of landscapes, a lot of still lifes, lots of royal portraits, and lots and lots of 1950s prints and '60s prints which I love [*laughs*], but there isn't a major Sutherland, for example. There are great artists that are represented by prints but not the real thing. Is that to do with money?

PJ: No Freud, apart from an interesting early landscape. No Bacons…

CP: There are some huge omissions.

AR: That's another question of course…

CP: Other public collections have very rich examples of those major British figures, like Bacon and Sutherland. The GAC has got the likes of John Bratby (fig.99), which I love, but there's only a Freud painting…

PJ: No Turner original.

CP: No Turner original. That's amazing.

PJ: A John Constable portrait – no landscape. You think of British artists, you think they would be…

CP: There are many omissions… there are lots of duplicates but not much meat on the bones of the 20th century…

AR: But there may be a variety of reasons for those omissions. There's the obvious practical one, which is an economic issue, but I think there may be other reasons why things are not on the radar at a certain moment, and by the time they are on the radar…

CP: They become too expensive.

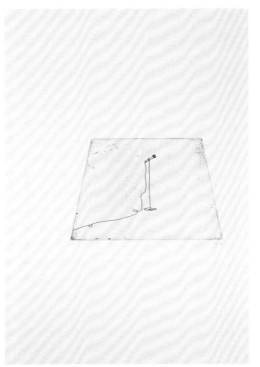

fig.96
David Shrigley
Untitled (Microphone), 2005
Soft-ground etching

fig.97
David Shrigley
Untitled (Matchstick figures), 2005
Soft-ground etching

fig.98
Grayson Perry
Print for a Politician, 2005
Etching

fig.99
John Bratby
*Window, Dartmouth Row,
Blackheath, c.1954–56*
Oil on hardboard

AR: They become too expensive and it's not appropriate any more.

CP: They are exhibited in non-museum conditions – I don't know if that makes any difference. I was a bit disappointed in terms of heavy hitters in the Collection. There are some really nice idiosyncratic things by those artists, but not the real gems I was looking for. Perhaps there would have been too much competition for those… when you think of the Arts Council Collection or the British Council Collection, or the National Gallery, which have prime examples of our best artists. Somehow their role as an ambassador hasn't been seized on by the GAC – our best work should be going out into the world. But that's all down to who was curating at the time, or the amount of money available, so it's hard to know. And also the sheer number of places you have to furnish. Hence the multiples, hence buying big print collections.

AR: But the things that you're pointing to that are missing are, in a strange sort of way, less essential because they're represented in museums by definition. I'm not saying that this collection should be non-museum work – on the contrary, there are many works in the Collection that are clearly of museum standing, and the museums that borrow them would attest to that. But because of its quirky nature maybe that's not where we should be looking. I'm wondering if there are other kinds of gaps that are not at the Francis Bacon level. Actually, I think it would have been a quirk if there *had* been a Francis Bacon in the Collection.

fig.100
Tracey Emin
The Simple Truth, 1995
Wool, cotton and felt
Arts Council Collection England

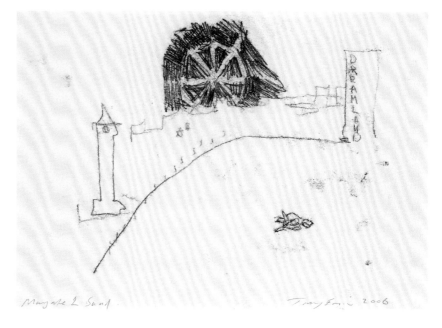

fig.101
Tracey Emin
Margate 1 Sand, 2006
Monoprint

fig.102
Tracey Emin
Still Love You Margate, 2006
Monoprint

CP: When I was on the Arts Council Collection panel in 1997, we bought an early Tracey Emin quilt, quite cheaply on the secondary market. It reads *Tracey Emin: Here to Stay* and features an American flag (fig.100). That seemed a work that could easily be in this collection. I'm not saying that we should buy lots of Tracey Emins… but it had different meanings obviously, depending on which bed it was thrown over, or which wall it was hung on. There are a few works in the Collection that do that, that have a charge that can electrify a space. But I think those kinds of works weren't being bought for the GAC until recently. I was looking for something more dark and dangerous and more pithy, and perhaps there are a few such works latent within the Collection, but there's a lot of stuff round them which is not.

PJ: It's interesting with Tracey, we have a couple of her prints now (figs 101 and 102). They are very Tracey because of the drawing style, and the fact they're monoprints of Margate showing landmarks such as the Ferris wheel and the clock tower. There's a tiny drawing of what looks like a couple copulating on the beach. It's interesting that we can show this now… Previously so much of what she did wouldn't go on the walls anywhere. People wouldn't take it. Things have definitely shifted.

CP: Well, it's come full circle from the political cartoonists of yesteryear. Now Grayson Perry has taken on that mantle in a very robust way. And I think people really enjoy it, it's like having the joker in the court. I do think quite a few of these artists, like the ones I mentioned before – Shrigley and Parr – slip under the radar and they're very effective in those political contexts, but it's the humour that allows them to slip by.

PJ: It's also very complex because I actually think that, in general, people's interest in art is greater than it was 20 years ago.

CP: And politicians' interest in art must have grown.

AR: There's an authority to the idea of the contemporary that never existed before, I think. We used to look to history for authority but today we look for something contemporary, and we have faith in artists and contemporary artists. We're looking at this Michael Landy drawing [documenting the destruction of his possessions] (fig.103) as an example; it's a self-conscious drawing, it's a drawing about him and it's about his history. Where he fits in. It is incidentally a drawing about Britishness; it's certainly a drawing about a British artist trying to piece together his life after an extraordinary moment. And we're more interested in artists now than we ever were.

CP: That's one of the ones I want to see in the flesh.

fig.103
Michael Landy
Compulsory Obsolescence, 2002
Pen and ink on paper

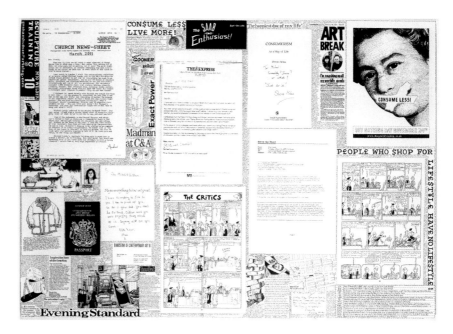

AR: It's incredible; it's an obsessive piece, like so many of Michael's recent works.

CP: Beautiful, great.

AR: Beautiful, but kind of crazy.

CP: Have you got any portraits of politicians by him? *[laughs]*

PJ: No. He's said he's not doing any more portraits. I just wanted to add that about five years ago we had kept some money back to buy a work by Gilbert and George. But that all fell through so I looked at our collection to see what was missing from it. I realised we didn't have a Damien Hirst. Whatever you think of him, I felt it was something that we would be expected to have. That's when we bought the spot painting, which we purchased for a reasonable amount – we couldn't have a formaldehyde because of the conservation challenges, but the spot paintings are very iconic works.

CP: Yes, those spots seem to have permeated popular culture everywhere. YBA [Young British Artists] art has sold for a huge amount of money – even the Tate's lost out to private collectors, richer museums overseas and Saatchi. So it's been very hard for any public collection to buy those works. British art is very much known throughout the world, it is our greatest export. When you think of all the British embassies all over the world that could be furnished with them…

AR: But let's look at where the strengths are. There clearly are fantastic paintings in the Collection, and still what the Collection does is expose you to stuff that you wouldn't normally take on board. We were talking about the painting that we just looked at – David Roberts's painting of Jerusalem (fig.104). What's fantastic about it is that it's not necessarily a painting that you might seek out, but you totally understand why it's in this collection.

CP: I think what's great about the Collection is the cumulative history of the object, the history of where it's been, and its role as a British ambassador. I was curious to look at how you have ended up with the work that you have in the Collection and the different reasons for that… There are of course paintings that have been chosen for their depiction of history.

AR: And it's a reflection of a very particular perspective of history…

CP: Yes.

AR: … so the landscape that you look at is…

CP: … framed by the victor! [Laughs.]

AR: Yes, you can say that, exactly. He, inevitably he who observes, is viewing from a very particular perspective. That kind of view of Jerusalem strikes me as more than symbolic. It's the Englishman who goes out on his quest into his symbolic landscape – he actually has to go into a real landscape.

fig.104
David Roberts
View of Jerusalem from the Mount of Olives, 1855
Oil on canvas

fig.105
Susan Collins
Seascape, Stokes Bay, 18th October
2008 at 18.44pm, 2008
Digital inkjet print on
Photorag paper

CP: So whether it's an image of the Wailing Wall or a painting of Poets' Corner in Westminster Abbey, there is a sense of the recording of particular histories that the Collection has homed in on. Now, with more recently acquired contemporary work, the other side of the wall is being shown.

AR: I have this fantasy that artworks are influential, that they change your state of being, that they might actually make you think again. What's very clear is that a lot of GAC works that are installed today are far more than decoration. You cannot *not* notice them. They don't just recede into the background.

CP: The contemporary work in the Collection is operating in a whole different way. Protocols have dropped away somewhat as we don't live in such a class-ridden society.

PJ: Abroad, diplomats always like to have works that have connections with the place. This helps to emphasise cultural commonalities either in historical or in contemporary terms and it's clear they become conversation pieces.

CP: We were talking about how history painting is very well represented in the Collection. Now there's almost a contemporary mapping going on with Grayson Perry, Kathy Prendergast or Darren Almond…

PJ: … and Susan Collins's digital landscapes (fig.105) – where she set up webcams to record the passing of time at five key locations along the south-east coast of England…

CP: Maps seem a very traditional ambassadorial thing to have – the map on the wall. I love the way it's being redrawn all the time, in a more fantastical way. There are also a lot of contemporary text-based works.

AR: That's a very interesting question because of course the use of language – the written word – is a phenomenon in recent art, and English is such an issue because of its universality. It does lead us to a kind of laziness in terms of our relationship to English. It's very interesting when an artist brings language into the frame – it does sort of bring you back, it is sometimes quite surprising…

CP: There's a Hamish Fulton I'm looking at called *No Talking For Seven Days* (fig.106). *[Laughs.]*

AR: But of course he's a landscape artist as well, so he fits our other category… Can I push you on where we began, as I want to see if you can reframe it a little? One of the aspects that I find interesting in your own work is that part of your practice is curatorial, that you bring things together in a particular way. And the works that you bring to display always have a backstory – there's always a history. Either that history is one that you have contributed to, or it's one that you found, so the thing that's in front of you is really only the surface of it, and there are layers and layers and layers of history behind it. I guess that's why you're the perfect person to look at this collection! But I'm wondering, at the risk of answering the same question again, if I can ask you what your methodology would be, in terms of selection. Do you wallow around in it for a while or is there a way that you enter it?

fig.106
Hamish Fulton
No Talking for Seven Days from the portfolio *Ten Toes Towards the Rainbow*, 1993
Screenprint

CP: I think for me all my work is very intuitive. I don't go in with the great master plan. And I do wallow around in it, and patterns emerge. I've gone through the Collection and just chosen things I like visually, and then started to think, well actually perhaps I should do it the other way round, I should look at what other people have chosen, what Margaret Thatcher or Tony Blair or Churchill chose to have in their more private quarters, diplomatic quarters. And see where those meet. But it's been a big trawl and you have to process a lot of information. Then I thought, well, perhaps I'll just show 20 double portraits of George V and his consort and that would be the show. So I can think of very radical approaches to curating that might shed very little light on the Collection but might reveal a little glimpse of my personal fetishism. I'm trying to seek out hidden corners of work that have been chosen over time by so many people from different sides of the political divide. So at the moment I'm still halfway through the process.

AR: But you don't need to be responsible. There is that sense if you're trying to make an exhibition around the Government Art Collection that there's almost no way to make a responsible selection… So the only way for you to work presumably is for you to go to the hidden corners of the invisible parts.

CP: It's all about looking in the end. It'll become clearer as I wade through but I think at the moment things are jumping out at me as anomalies and in a way perhaps that's it… Maybe it'll be a collection of anomalies…

AR: Shall we talk about your work in the Collection?

CP: I want to talk briefly about this one piece I have in the Collection called *Up Down Charm Strange* (fig.107), which consists of six photograms of feathers. There's a feather that's been to the top of Everest in the jacket of Rebecca Stevens who was the first British woman to climb Everest. There's a feather that went to the South Pole in Sir Ranulph Fiennes's sleeping bag; a feather out of Sigmund Freud's pillow, off his couch; a feather from a wandering albatross, which I got from the Antarctic Survey. There's a feather from Benjamin Franklin's attic (which looks like a kite) and then a raven feather from the Tower of London. The popular myth is that if the ravens ever leave the Tower then the monarchy will fall, so I just took a small feather! Feathers… seem to crop up a lot in my work – the idea of defying gravity, offset by the idea of Icarus falling… I used the feathers trapped in a glass slide then put them in a photographic enlarger to make photograms. They are quiet contemplative works. Most of these feathers have been hidden in a pillow or a sleeping bag or a jacket and they haven't seen the light of day for a long time. They have all got their histories but then they end

fig.107
Cornelia Parker
Feather that went to the Top of Everest [In the jacket of Rebecca Stevens, the first British woman to climb Mt. Everest]

Feather that went to the South Pole [In the sleeping bag of Sir Ranulph Fiennes on his trip across Antarctica]

Feather from Benjamin Franklin's Attic [With thanks to the Benjamin Franklin Museum]

Feather from Freud's Pillow [From his couch] [With thanks to the Freud Museum]

Raven Feather from the Tower of London

Feather from a Wandering Albatross [With thanks to the British Antarctic Survey, Cambridge]

Photograms from the series
Up Down Charm Strange,
1997–98

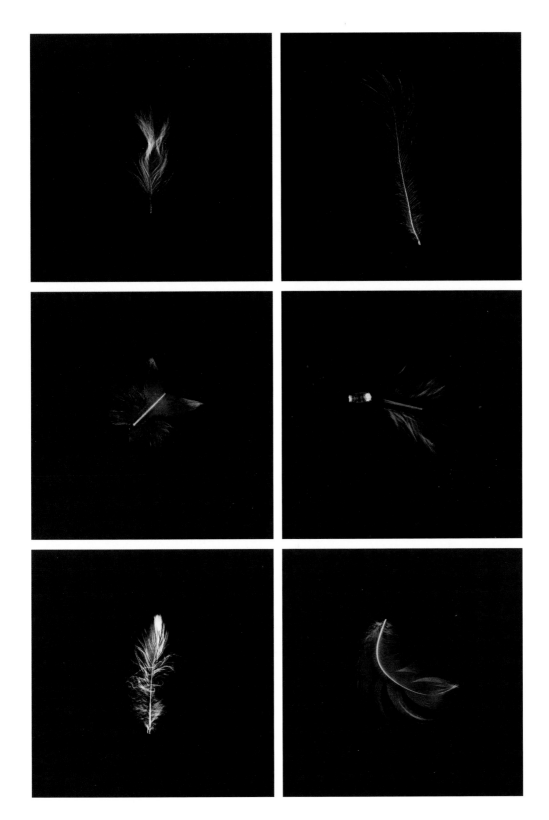

up in the little dark wood-panelled dining room used by Gordon Brown at Number 11 for several years. I think these works chimed well with his interest in bravery and derring-do…

PJ: They were also most recently in Barbara Follett's office when she was Minister for Culture.

CP: It is great that they are just going off and doing their thing. Like my line of squashed silver in the British Ambassador's Residence, Paris, in that context I'm sure it has a very different resonance… but then some of the works in the Collection have been commissioned for specific places, haven't they? Has that commissioning happened throughout the centuries?

PJ: There has been commissioning since the Collection began… at first it was the copying of portraits and then the first main commission in 1949 was John Piper.

CP: There was a lot around the Coronation wasn't there?

PJ: Yes, Lowry and a number of other artists – probably the largest number of artists commissioned at any one time by us. We occasionally commission artists to make work for the Collection – Catherine Yass (figs 139 and 140), Andrew Grassie (figs 108 and 109)…

CP: Yes, the Andrew Grassie I particularly like – the one of your store rooms.

PJ: Juxtaposed with Number 10.

CP: I like that and the fact that he's got THINGS by Martin Creed in the painting, and I'd love to be able to borrow both those things together.

PJ: Would it be interesting to do a whole exhibition of what's been in the sculpture store?

CP: Yes, I was looking at all those but sadly some of them are a bit boring.

PJ: Oh yes, you commented about being a bit disappointed in the sculpture. There's a challenge with sculpture in that it's more difficult to place – there are always more walls in an office and less floor space as such… Most of our sculpture tends to be commissioned or we acquire large pieces and they go straight on display. Are there any particular works that you'd highlight in the Collection?

fig.108
Andrew Grassie
*The Government Art Collection
Sculpture Store*, 2002
Tempera on paper

fig.109
Andrew Grassie
*The Pillared Room at 10 Downing
Street*, 2002
Tempera on paper

CP: The ones I'd choose are probably the ones you have highlighted yourself. There's a Craigie Aitchison (fig.110)… I love the Basil Beattie [*Loose Ends*] and the Chris Ofili [*Portmadog 14/9/96*] and the Bomberg, the Armenian church [*Jerusalem, Interior of the Armenian Church*]. It's funny – I quite like a painting by Winston Churchill (fig.111).

AR: I drive past the Home Office every day and see the Liam Gillick work as it protrudes from the building (fig.143). Like so much of Liam's work, it is the site that provokes conversation. He creates a space in which you might develop a discourse. So it's actually an extreme animation of what

fig.111
Winston Spencer Churchill
Mimizan Lake, c.1922
Oil on canvas

fig.110
Craigie Aitchison
Portrait of Alton Peters, 1983
Oil on canvas

every work of art in the Collection should do; it should be the provocation for an extended series of conversations. It is just that he frames it. And I also think that is something true of the Collection as a whole. So often you don't know it's there because it's so embedded in what you think of and what you cherish and value in terms of our culture. Whether it's images that are super, super familiar to us like the portrait of Lord Byron or… I am just looking here at the Angelica Kauffmann portrait by Daniel Gardner (fig.112). That's also very important because of what kind of representation might take place. Here's this strong self-defining woman who is being represented in the Collection through a portrait of herself and, as stylised as it is, and as 18th-century as it is as a painting, dated 1773, it also feels incredibly contemporary in terms of the agenda of the painting. That is something I feel can be applied to much of the Collection. That is why I don't feel it is an accident that [here on this table] the image is juxtaposed with the great hero of contemporary British art – Bridget Riley.

PJ: It is no accident!

CP: If I had to pick out highlights, Bridget Riley is somebody I hugely admire – even the two prints you have are wonderful.

PJ: We have two original works on paper as well as a painting.

CP: So those are the ways…

PJ: In 2008 we also managed to acquire a Stanley Spencer because it wasn't quite as finished as his works normally are. We got it for £25,000 and most of his work goes for much more. If you look critically at that painting you can see that it is not one of his major works, but because of the cultural links it's perfect for our purposes. It shows the Ming tombs just outside Beijing (fig.113) – Spencer went out to China in 1952 as part of a cultural delegation. And it's unusual because Stanley Spencer hardly ever went abroad.

CP: Yes I know – Stanley Spencer in China is quite mind-blowing as an idea.

AR: The irony is that the Government Art Collection is able to tell alternative histories to the textbook, and you'd think it would be the Collection that would have told the official story. It actually flips it…

CP: … and tells the unofficial story.

fig.112
Daniel Gardner
Portrait of Angelica Kauffmann,
RA (1741–1807), Painter, c.1773
Oil on canvas

fig.113
Stanley Spencer
The Ministers, Ming Tombs, Peking,
1954
Oil on canvas

AR: That's mind-blowing in terms of the GAC's remit. The 'official' representation of Britishness is, in effect, an alternative take!

CP: It's like Chris Ofili producing etchings about Wales, which I think is about as crazy as Stanley Spencer going to China.

PJ: There was something else you said which made me think of another statistic about us that is unusual – that two-thirds of our Collection works are out on display at any one time. So if we buy a contemporary work, the chances are it will be out on display and thousands of people will see it.

CP: People of influence?

PJ: Yes, people of influence but also people who might not necessarily have seen much art…

CP: … and therefore it becomes a much more charged space, an activated space, for art to exist in. People who go to museums are going there voluntarily to look at art – but you've got a captive audience for

fig.114
Gillian Wearing
Dancing in Peckham
(production still), 1994/97
R-type photograph

fig.115
John Wood and Paul Harrison
Slide from the series Twenty Six
(Drawing and Falling Things),
2000–01
Video

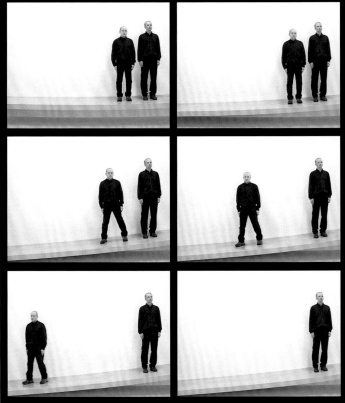

this collection. It's a wonderful opportunity for contemporary artists to be out in the world in these rarified circles that not many people have access to.

PJ: Rarified because lots of people don't have ready access, but in fact lots of people do go in to visit.

CP: They are highly charged situations quite often – many important political moments have taken place in front of GAC works – but... being active in the world is what most artists would hope for, for their work, having their own future... That's what I find fascinating... I wonder what Ed Miliband's chosen?

PJ: I didn't see him when he made his selection, but he doesn't get anything now because if you are in opposition you don't, not even if you are the leader. Only those that are in power.

CP: Oh, is that true? Wow!

PJ: Only those who are in power.

CP: And how do you show video works? Like Gillian Wearing's *Dancing in Peckham* (fig.114)?

PJ: Generally on a monitor. They don't go out as much but they do go. We've got a Wood and Harrison set of five currently in DCMS [Department of Culture, Media and Sport] (fig.115).

AR: Weren't they in Number 10 before?

PJ: Yes, it was great to get them into Number 10.

AR: It was fantastic. They just looked bonkers in there.

CP: The idea of them being transplanted into a political situation is wonderful... they have a multiplicity of readings as they come into contact with so many movers and shakers in a way that transcends the art itself.

PJ: Well that's interesting. When I arrived and I wanted to put photography into Number 10 we weren't allowed to. It took – I can't remember when the first one went in – maybe four or five years... and then to get video in! The next thing should be a live performance!

fig.116
Richard Wilson
The Cock Inn, Cheam Common,
c.1745–47
Oil on canvas

fig.117
Francis Cotes
Sir William Chambers (1726–1796)
Architect, c.1764
Oil on canvas

fig.118
David Roberts
(Lithographer Louis Haghe)
Interview with the Viceroy of
Egypt at his Palace, Alexandria,
May 12th 1839
Hand-coloured lithograph,
published 1849

fig.119
Cosmo Clark
Circus Scene, 1936
Verre églomisé (oil on glass)

5. PAPER LEAVES AND CONCRETE TREES: THE DIPLOMATIC ART OF COMMISSIONING

Adrian George

> The trouble with embassies is that most of what they do is barely distinguishable from the activities of a conventional office building. Most of the work takes place in small cellular rooms. And yet we expect them to feel as special as the palace that Wellington acquired for Britain in Paris.
> – Deyan Sudjic, 2000[1]

Not all government buildings are as grand as the 18th-century palace of Pauline Borghese (sister of Napoleon Bonaparte) that was acquired for the nation by the 1st Duke of Wellington in 1814 and has been home to the British embassy in Paris ever since. Nevertheless, the expectation is that they should all be impressive while remaining functional, for they must represent Britain, promoting its history, culture and aims. One of the ways the Government Art Collection (GAC) has helped to manage this expectation is by the appropriate placement of works of art from the Collection. What is less well known is that the GAC commissions.

Commissioning by government departments can be traced back to the 19th and early 20th centuries when a growing number of artists, many of whom made their living as professional copyists, responded to the State's demand for paintings of monarchs and princes.[2] The need for manual copying slowly died out and the nature of the art market changed gradually too, with a larger role being played by artists' representatives, galleries and dealers. Connoisseurship also developed, with more emphasis being placed on the quality of art-making and the intellectual aspects of works of art rather than the materials used.

During both world wars, what had been the burgeoning economies of the commercial art market all but ceased. As a result, and due to a perceived need to ensure the survival of British artistic cultural identity during both wartime and the inter-war years, the Government established a number of schemes that employed artists in the war effort. Several commissioning projects were run during World War I, with the majority of artworks produced going directly into the collection of the newly established Imperial War Museum.

With the onset of World War II, Kenneth Clark, then director of the National Gallery and Surveyor of the King's Pictures, did his utmost to ensure that many British artists were not lost. His stated that his intention was 'simply to keep artists at work under any pretext, and, as far as

fig.120
John Piper
Cheltenham: Composite of Houses in Priory Parade and Elsewhere, 1949
Oil on canvas

possible, to prevent them from being killed'.[3] Clark suggested that a pictorial record of the war be made to which as many artists as possible would contribute, each providing an insight that mere documentation could not (fig.121).

By 1945 some 5,570 works of art accumulated under the War Artists scheme were catalogued and then distributed. Large public museums were given priority, with the majority of works going to the Tate and the British Council Collections. Although the Government Art Collection was not directly involved in the scheme, 169 pieces by important artists such as Edward Bawden, Bernard Hailstone, William Coldstream and Carel Weight were allocated to the GAC's parent department, the Ministry of Works, for display in government buildings and remain part of the Collection to this day.

In 1949 the Ministry of Works took a significant step forward in commissioning an artist to create works specific to a new building: the British embassy in the then capital of Brazil, Rio de Janeiro. The architect, Scottish-born Robert Russell Prentice,[4] created a traditional building in the 18th-century neoclassical Adam style,[5] incorporating a number of wall panels into the smaller dining room (fig.122). Although these were considered ideal locations for works of art, the Foreign Office felt the cost of purchasing existing works of such great dimensions might be excessive.

The newly appointed Richard Walker,[6] part-time government art advisor, working with colleagues at the Ministry, proposed a commission as a more cost-effective way of providing art to fill the panels:

fig.121
Paul Nash, official war artist, sketching at the Cowley aircraft dump outside Oxford, 1944

fig.122
The British Embassy in Rio de Janeiro, photographed in 1951

The question of the decoration of the large panels in the dining room of the new Embassy at Rio de Janeiro was also discussed. It was agreed that it would be absurd if the Treasury tried to make us provide for the needs in pictures of a new building on the grand scale, such as this one, out of the ordinary picture fund [at that time £1,000 per annum]. Several possibilities were considered and it was decided that there were many advantages to commissioning a modern artist to do a series of paintings especially for these panels. You kindly agreed to ask Mr. John Piper how much he would charge for such a series of paintings.[7]

John Piper was an extraordinarily prolific artist and had come to wider public attention through his work as an official war artist.[8] His body of work encapsulated painting, printmaking, writing and illustration, as well as book, poster and textile designs, theatre and costume designs and even stained-glass windows. Piper sat on numerous advisory bodies and in 1946 became a trustee of the Tate Gallery. He had a great deal of experience of working to commission, and his neo-Romantic style seemed in tune with the Government's ideas of representing British heritage abroad.

Contemporary newspaper reports[9] suggest that the subject matter had been given to the artist, but records show that Piper was, in fact, provided with little more than the dimensions of the wall space available for his works (152.4 x 213.4 cm). With this information the artist set about his work. His designs, in yellows, oranges, magentas and blues, took as their starting point the Regency architecture of the spa towns of Bath, Brighton and Cheltenham (figs 120 and 123–126). In turn this reflected the Regency-style interiors of the proposed embassy 'in dramatic colour with strong sunlight and shadow effects. They are considered by some experts to be the finest work which this artist has yet produced.'[10]

Piper presented the finished works at a special exhibition at the Victoria and Albert Museum in November 1949, just before the paintings were shipped to Brazil:[11] 'Mr Piper's hot colour – brilliant yellow façades and undulating balconies have every appearance of fantastic stage settings from a land of architectural make-believe.'[12]

A year later his gouache design drawings appeared in the first exhibition of the Society of Mural Painters. Organised by the Arts Council of Great Britain, the display opened at the New Burlington Galleries, London, and later toured England. The accompanying pamphlet included a 'price per square foot' for murals, should one wish to commission one of the artists. Piper received £200 per painting for Rio, a significant amount of money at the time (fig.127).

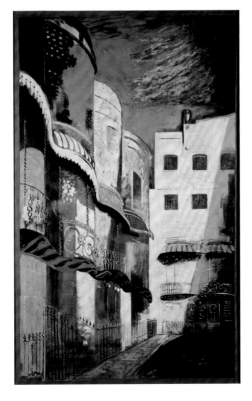

fig.127
The 'Private Dining Room' at the British Embassy, Rio de Janeiro, 1951, showing three of the five works by John Piper *in situ*

figs 123–126
(clockwise from top left)
John Piper
Cheltenham: Montpelier Walk, 1949

Bath: Composite of Bath Street and Corner of Camden Crescent, 1949

Bath: Grosvenor Crescent, 1949

Brighton: Regency Square, 1949
Oil on canvas

Ten years later Brasilia was inaugurated as the new capital of Brazil. Although there was a British representative in the capital from that point, the embassy did not move fully until 1973. Two years later the Piper works were still in Rio, with questions being asked about what should happen to them.[13] A year later the decision was made to split the group up and they have never been shown together since.[14]

In 1953 Sir David Eccles, then Minister for Works, in collaboration with Richard Walker, commissioned several artists, many of them previously official war artists, to make artworks relating to the Coronation of Queen Elizabeth II on 2 June that year. His intention was to show 'what our contemporary artists have made of the Coronation'.[15] This project led to 30 works finding their way into the GAC by artists such as Edward Ardizzone, Edward Bawden, Richard Eurich, Laura Knight, Leonard Rosoman (fig.128) and Carel Weight. It was thought that a book of images of the works produced could be sold to raise funds for the purchase of more works of art for display in government buildings in Britain and abroad. Sadly, the book never materialised; nor did the much-needed funds.

Amongst the artists commissioned by the Ministry of Works was L. S. Lowry. Although Lowry had previously been commissioned by the War Artists Advisory Committee,[16] he was astounded to be asked to be an official Coronation artist. His own work, he believed, depicted the gritty realism of his northern working-class upbringing, so he could

fig.128
Leonard Rosoman
The Coronation Procession in the Mall, from Admiralty Arch, 1953
Watercolour and gouache on paper

not understand why he was invited to commemorate such a grand occasion. He nevertheless travelled to London, staying there with a relative. He wrote about his experience to his artist friend David Carr:

> I did all right on the day last week. I fear I didn't get there as early as I ought to have done (six o'clock in the morning was the time they asked folk to be in their places and I would hate to tell you what time I did arrive). The weather was awful in the afternoon, not so terrible in the morning. I was perched in a stand in front of the Palace – a very good view – in fact it couldn't have been better. What I am going to paint I don't know.[17]

fig.129
Laurence Stephen Lowry sketching

It seems once again that the ministry gave little in terms of direction as to what the artist might paint; in the same letter Lowry notes: 'Some excellent incidents took place around about which fascinated me but not, I should imagine, what the Ministry of Works want, I am sorry to say.'[18]

Although Lowry had taken a sketch pad with him he made no drawings on the day of the Coronation. Instead, he returned the following day, producing several sketches but still with no idea of what exactly to paint (fig.129). By the end of July he had almost completed what for him was 'a straightforward view from [his] seat at the top of the Mall' (fig.130).[19] By August the work was finished and dispatched, the artist was paid £100 for the painting (and its copyright) and informed that the work was destined for the British embassy in Moscow.

fig.130
Laurence Stephen Lowry
The Procession passing the Queen Victoria Memorial, Coronation, 1953
Oil on canvas

Lowry was delighted by the news of its destination: 'They think I'm a Communist, because I paint what I do.'[20] Two years later he was offered an OBE in the Queen's Birthday Honours, but politely declined.[21] He also declined a CBE, and in 1967 a knighthood, stating then, 'All my life I have felt most strongly against social distinctions of any kind... I hope you will understand my feelings when I regretfully say that I feel I must graciously decline this honour.'[22]

In 1970 the Ministry of Works became part of the Department of the Environment. Two years later many responsibilities for the Collection were transferred to the largely autonomous Property Services Agency (PSA).[23] In 1974 the PSA made the decision to commission a small number of artists to produce original works for reproduction as multiple prints that could then be used in many government buildings (including

159

hospitals, universities and even post offices) and fine art limited editions. The intention was to engage in a meaningful programme of art displays in publicly accessible areas of government buildings.[24] It was concluded that multiple prints would be made 'by well known modern British Artists and Limited Editions produced by younger British Artists who are on or approaching the threshold of a wider recognition'.[25] Two years later the programme was under way with artists Robyn Denny, Eduardo Paolozzi, Tom Phillips (who replaced Ben Nicholson) and William Scott (fig.131) all approached to produce multiples. Nigel Hall (fig.132), Derek Hirst, Ben Johnson, Bert Kitchen and Norman Stevens (who replaced David Inshaw) were selected to make limited editions.

Editions Alecto (EA)[26] were invited to tender for the production of as many as 2,500 copies of selected prints for government use and, while the ministry held the copyright, EA would have exclusive rights to produce and sell unlimited copies. The Department of the Environment also stood to make 7.5 per cent on any commercial sales of copies EA

fig.131
William Scott
Blue Still Life, 1975
Watercolour on paper

fig.132
Nigel Hall
Dialogue, 1975
Aquatint

made. The limited edition prints were produced in editions of 125, of which the department purchased 75 and EA retained the rest for sale.

Hundreds of the 'multiple prints' were supplied to locations around the UK and overseas. Being intentionally low-value works, in effect reproductions, they were not tracked or inventoried after dispatch and were regarded as more or less disposable.[27] The limited-edition works, always intended for use by the Pictures Section of the Property Services Agency (which became the GAC), remained and still form part of the current Collection.

The commissioning project was abandoned after two years. Many artists and galleries were producing limited-edition prints which could be bought ad hoc and probably at lower cost. The Ministry felt that there was no advantage in commissioning artists to make original works for reproduction other than to be seen as a patron – which was not its intention.

While the 'multiples' project was laudable in many ways, the result was disappointing. Other commissioning projects, however, were significantly more successful. It was under the auspices of the PSA that the Queen Elizabeth II Conference Centre in Westminster was built. A new government building had been proposed for the site for some time, but plans remained in limbo until a feasibility study was drawn up in 1975. The Centre was eventually built to a design by Powell & Moya Architects and opened by the Queen in 1986.

fig.133
Mary Restieaux
Ikat Weave Hanging: East and *Ikat Weave Hanging: West*, 1985–86
Silk ikat weaving

As soon as information on the conference centre became available, the then curator of the GAC, Dr Wendy Baron, contacted the architects and initiated informal discussions about the inclusion of works of art in the new building. The PSA formalised this engagement in 1983. Site visits ensued, and in October that year Dr Baron wrote to Lord Gowrie, Minister for the Arts, asking him to consider allocating a percentage of the construction cost to the provision of artworks for the building.[28] A few days later, Lord Gowrie wrote to the Secretary of State for the Environment, Patrick Jenkin (who delegated responsibility through the PSA), to 'see if some positive steps could be taken to allot a small percentage of building budgets for works of art… I believe that if we were to do so the Government would gain great credit for this, give a boost to the opportunities for individual artists and create something of a shop window for the larger sale of their work.'[29]

In his response Jenkin made no commitment but commented that 'generally, at a time of expenditure restraint, we need to be sensitive

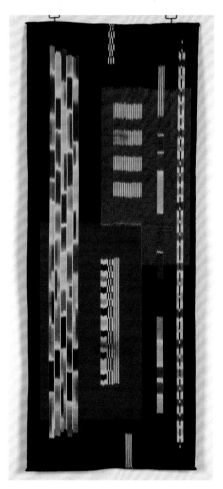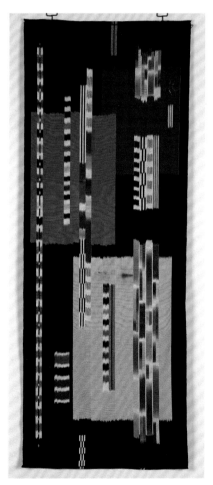

fig.134
John Dugger
Time-Zones, 1986
Felt wall banner

to the public view which tends to regard works of art, especially if they take an abstract form, as unnecessary extravagance... For reasons of this kind I do not think it would be wise to go beyond the modest existing delegations from the Treasury.'[30] Nevertheless, by November 1984, a proposal was on the table for around 200 works to be purchased, lent or commissioned. Amongst them textiles by Mary Restieaux, a silk mosaic by Lucienne Day, paintings by Patrick Heron and Craigie Aitchison, wall hangings by Restieaux (fig.133), Caroline Slinger and John Dugger (fig.134) and a large, site-specific installation by Eduardo Paolozzi. Altogether £162,000 was committed for the acquisition (through purchase or commission) of works of art for what was to be a landmark building.

By this time Paolozzi had a significant international reputation – he had exhibited his work widely, was a Royal Academician, lecturer at the Royal College of Art and professor in Munich. His previous works were taken into consideration and Lord Gowrie was keen to see a distinctive work by this artist in the new building. The suites and main rooms of the building had been named after famous British political or cultural figures, such as Mountbatten and Churchill. The site proposed for Paolozzi was the Benjamin Britten Lounge.

Commissioning contracts were researched (with reference made to articles by leading art law expert Henry Lydiate), drafted and reviewed by contract managers. For the first time the Government was not looking to acquire the copyright of the work at the point of commissioning. The artist was given a specific location and dimensions to work to, a schedule and a staged payment plan.

163

fig.135
Eduardo Paolozzi sitting in front
of his sculptural relief *On This Island*,
1986

fig.136
Eduardo Paolozzi
*On This Island (after Benjamin
Britten Op.11)*, 1985–86
Wood

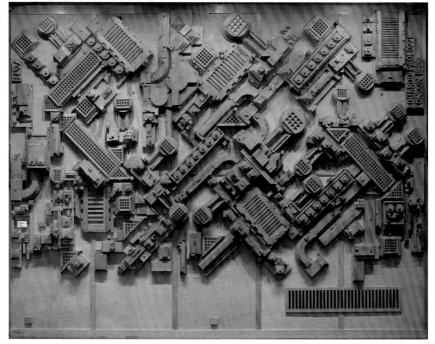

164

Paolozzi's work, a wall-based wooden bas-relief of just over 29 square metres, is titled *On this Island* and references aspects of Paolozzi's life and interests (fig.135).[31] It takes as its starting point a song cycle by Britten, based on a poem by W. H. Auden, both of which Paolozzi had appreciated as a student. Paolozzi explained:

> *On This Island* began while the conference centre was in early stages of construction with a preliminary creation of a basic 'alphabet' of shapes… Similar motifs juxtaposed to create a cluster might suggest a chord of music, to be repeated elsewhere at a different scale with a different surround. Spaces suggest a silent pause. The viewer's mind may be engaged in making varied connections between form and music – an activity well recorded in the history of art.[32]

The work was intended to be seen and read from different distances and angles. Each view of the work, Paolozzi thought, might allow a different interpretation – at close proximity the intricate workings of a giant clock, from further away some sort of pre-Industrial Revolution machinery, and from a distance a universal utopian landscape. Even though the work was fully installed by the time of the royal opening (24 June 1986), some small adjustments were made to the work a day or so later when additional elements were added and the wood finally sealed against possible staining (fig.136).

Compared with the GAC's practices today, it seems that little thought went into the work's future care prior to its being installed, as it was two months after the work had been completed that a cleaning and maintenance document was sent out. At the time, all the projects at the Conference Centre were seen as extremely successful. Over the years, however, all works other than Paolozzi's have been removed, either because building managers felt they were unwanted or because they were not able to care for them adequately.

Commissioning continued on and off over the next decade. Works were produced for the British high commission in Bangladesh, the British embassy in Dublin and, in 1996, for the British high commission in Canberra. A year later the newly appointed GAC director, Penny Johnson, visited Moscow where a new British embassy was being built. Due to the scale of the buildings and, in some instances, the challenging locations for displaying works of art, the only way forward was to commission new and site-specific work.

The GAC approached artists Langlands and Bell, Michael Craig-Martin and Alex Hartley to create works specific to the new building.[33] Taking

advantage of the fact that the building was already accessible, some of the artists benefited from being able to visit and thus tailor their proposals closely to their chosen locations. Alex Hartley became the first GAC-commissioned artist to take full advantage of the architecture of the location by integrating his piece into the fabric of the building. Hartley's site-specific installation created an unreal yet believable illusion of space beyond the corridor in which it was placed (fig.137). The artist recalls:

> The site selected was above a flight of steps – a difficult location. Although the piece is entirely informed by the architecture I have to admit that I had always envisaged a work that would somehow carry the viewer outside the building itself. In a way the challenges of the location, and its restrictions, became a positive. I love a deadline and I love a challenge and this commission gave me both. It quickened the mind and at the same time allowed me to experiment, taking some risks and to some extent losing the full control, which I see as both a plus and a minus of studio-based practice.[34]

fig.137
Alex Hartley's site-specific sculpture *Untitled (Embassy)*, 2000, British embassy, Moscow

fig.138
The exterior of the British embassy, Berlin

In the same year, 1997, a meeting was held between the Foreign and Commonwealth Office (FCO), the GAC and the architect Michael Wilford with regard to commissioning art for the new British embassy planned for Berlin, the capital of the reunified Germany. With all parties keen to ensure the creation of signature works for the striking new building, the budget for artworks was to be between 0.5 per cent and 1 per cent of the build costs (build being estimated at £20 million). By August 1997 a budget for art was tabled at £120,000, which was considered woefully inadequate given the prestige of the new building (fig.138). Michael Wilford recalls:

> We had quite a lot of experience of designing and building galleries or museums… so hanging works or placing sculpture had always been a significant aspect of our work. For a representative building such as an embassy, the choice of work and the manner in which it is incorporated into the building is critical. So often in public buildings the art comes along after the building is finished and appears like a badge or trophies, stuck on the wall like moose heads, clearly an afterthought, clearly not integrated in the building. The right kind of art in the right kind of place can enhance a building significantly.[35]

By July 1999 there was no budget at all as it had become clear that the Private Finance Initiative (PFI)[36] would not fund the acquisition of

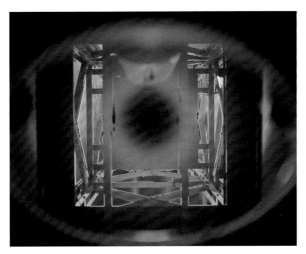

fig.139
Catherine Yass
Observatory, 2000
Colour transparency and light-box

fig.140
Catherine Yass
Pavilion, 2000
Colour transparency and light-box

artworks and the FCO had no funds either. This forced the Minister for the Arts to write to the Permanent Under-Secretary of the FCO:

> I would reiterate that it is vital for Britain's contribution to art, design and technology to be adequately represented in this new development at the heart of Europe, and it would be very sad if the only international project so far produced via the PFI scheme were to be bereft of such works of art owing to the scheme's deficiencies.[37]

Potential sites within the striking new building were considered by the architect and the GAC's director. In October 1999 proposals were presented to the GAC Advisory Committee along with an outline budget (subject to sponsorship) of £350,000. That month the GAC began to contact artists advising them that their commission was going to proceed.

Commissions began with Tony Cragg's *Dancing Columns* (fig.73), a two-part sculpture situated at the top of the main stairs to the embassy's atrium. Another British artist, Catherine Yass, was asked to make work that suggested links between the UK and Germany. Yass created two lightboxes in which she chose to photograph the interiors of buildings designed by the German architect Erich Mendelsohn – the Einstein Tower in Potsdam, Berlin and the De La Warr Pavilion in Bexhill-on-Sea, East Sussex (figs 139 and 140). The final work to be installed was on the rear wall of the atrium where the artist David Tremlett was invited to make a wall painting. Working with eight German art students over a two-week period, Tremlett applied pastel colours directly by hand onto the rear wall of the embassy. The colours and composition were influenced by Tremlett's travels in Africa and India.

The Moscow embassy opened in May 2000, with newspaper reports stating that 'the new British embassy in Moscow is dazzling Russians with its bold and spacious modern design'.[38] The Berlin embassy opened in July of the same year, with BBC News reporting that 'the new embassy was a symbol of vibrant British culture and the openness of British diplomacy'.[39] Both the Berlin and Moscow embassies were built in the period between the end of the Cold War and the terrorist attacks of 11 September 2001 – a period during which it was thought that open and accessible government buildings would be a positive way forward. Since that time, increased security measures have meant that most of these buildings have had to incorporate a significant 'stand-off' distance between the street and the offices, while public access has been limited.

In 1996 a project began to develop the site of the redundant Marsham Towers in Westminster (fig.141). Designed originally by Eric Bedford, the buildings had been home to the Department of the Environment but were increasingly unfit for purpose and inefficient to run. Nikolaus Pevsner's architectural guide *London 6: Westminster* notes that the buildings were 'the very image of faceless bureaucracy', and were often referred to as 'the three ugly sisters'. The towers were demolished in 2002–03 and the architect Terry Farrell, having won the design competition, began work on a new Home Office (fig.142). Again built under a PFI contract, the design was pared down to save on costs. However, the building was considered bland and uninteresting and attracted negative comments from the *Evening Standard's* architecture critic, Rowan Moore:

fig.141
The Department of the Environment, Marsham Towers, London, demolished in 2003

fig.142
A computer-designed model showing the original design for the Home Office, Terry Farrell & Partners

fig.144
The artist **Liam Gillick** (above) during a site visit to the Home Office, London

Such indifference can't be what the Prime Minister had in mind when… declaring his commitment to good design in public buildings. Uncontroversial though this statement might be (for who could wish our ministries, hospitals, schools and law courts to be badly designed?), it is impossible to imagine Thatcher or Major, or before them Callaghan, Wilson or Heath, saying this. Or, to judge by the Home Office, it occurring to Jack Straw that his ministry might be more than a machine in which to exert discipline.[40]

The then recently established Commission for Architecture and the Built Environment (CABE), having reviewed the plans for the building, proposed working with artists in order to create a distinct identity for the offices. In 2002 artist Liam Gillick was chosen by the GAC to work on enhancements to the façade of the building. His projects included replacing the planned concrete canopy with a coloured glass version, an entrance icon (fig.143), coloured vertical louvres in the ground-floor windows, two sculptural signs and a ceramic frit applied to the glass façade forming a 'hidden' text that wraps the entire building.[41] This was the first commissioning project for the GAC in the public realm, the first to deliver grand-scale artworks as architectural enhancements, and the first GAC-commissioned projects in London for 16 years.

Significant testing had to be carried out to ensure that Gillick's enhancements were durable and that they did not compromise the rigorous security measures employed in the building (fig.144). The Westminster Planning Department encouraged the PFI developer, Anne's Gate Property (AGP), to commission artwork for the new public spaces opened up by the building. With the active support and involvement of Home Office (HO) Minister Fiona MacTaggart and HO Permanent Secretary, Sir John Gieve, the GAC continued to be involved, working with Gillick, the HO and AGP to select and place work by six artists.

As well as the Deller and Kane project (discussed further on page 106), the GAC, with the HO, also commissioned Toby Paterson to create two murals for the entrance hall (figs 145 and 146). The projects were not without controversy. The Deller and Kane commission, *The Home Office Collection of Art from Prisons*, attracted some media attention, and it became clear that the press were not interested in the positive outcomes of art as rehabilitation, but were more concerned about the nominal fees paid for the works and the crimes committed by the offender-artists. This sparked interest in other arts projects in the building and the associated costs. In response to criticism, the HO felt it should be seen to be saving money wherever possible. With art an

fig.143
The entrance icon and coloured glass canopy of the Home Office, designed by artist **Liam Gillick** as enhancements to architect Terry Farrell's original design.

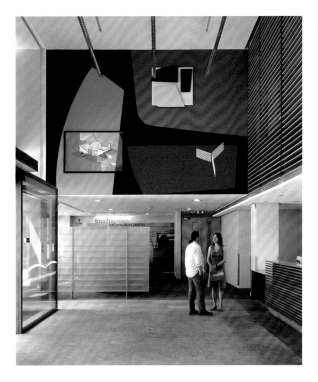

fig.145
Toby Paterson
*New Townscape 1 Triaxial
Axonometric*, 2005
Acrylic on perspex, acrylic on wood,
acrylic on wall, *in situ* at the Home
Office, London

fig.146
Toby Paterson
New Townscape 2 Civic Plan 2, 2005
Acrylic on perspex, acrylic on wood,
acrylic on walll, *in situ* at the Home
Office, London

easy target, the large metal sculpture proposed by Eva Rothschild was cancelled just a matter of weeks before it was due to be installed.

The final public project, proposed by Emma Kay, was to span a 25-year period of development and involved an annual open call to all UK citizens to submit short texts which would then be considered by an independent panel. A shortlist would then be drawn up, and those selected engraved on flagstones outside the HO building. The project ran successfully for one year, led by the GAC, after which the HO concluded that the project would have too great an impact on their staff time. The artist and the GAC looked for various solutions, but in 2009 it became clear that the project would have to be wound up. In spite of these disappointments, the HO building won several awards, including a nomination by the Royal Institute of British Architects in their 2005 RIBA Awards, and the Prime Minister's Better Public Building Award in which Gillick's enhancements to the building were specially mentioned.

In moving to their new premises, the HO left another building empty. Completed in 1976, 102 Petty France was originally designed by Sir Basil Spence;[42] however, in 2005 a full refurbishment began under the management of property developer Land Securities. The internal redesign provided more floor space, a new atrium and much improved staff facilities. Having seen the success of the commissioned works of art at the HO, the Department of Constitutional Affairs (now the Ministry of Justice) approached the GAC to commission work for their refurbished offices. After shortlisting, four artists went on to create projects: Martin Boyce, Lothar Götz, Conrad Shawcross and Nathaniel Rackowe (figs 147–150). Initially another four artists were also approached, but again concern over costs meant their projects did not proceed. A great deal of thought went into ensuring the commissioned works of art were robust and that environmental issues were addressed. Götz used a tough mineral paint more resistant to scratching than standard emulsions for his 51 wall paintings in the stairwells of the building. The wood used for Shawcross's five-storey spiralling sculpture came from renewable sources while Rackowe, working with an engineering company, ensured that his kinetic sculpture consumed as little energy as possible. The energy that was used was offset by reducing the number of ceiling lights in the area of the sculpture.

With all these projects the GAC has effectively, over the decades, been involved in arts patronage – either by supporting the work of emerging artists through direct purchase or through commissioning. However, government patronage of the arts is not without its challenges. With the slowing commercial art market and a dip in private patronage before, during and after the two world wars, the Government established the Council for the Encouragement of Music and the Arts (CEMA) to support, promote and maintain British culture. CEMA was to pave the way for the Arts Council of Great Britain (which in 1994 was then subdivided into the Arts Councils of England, Scotland and Wales). Although the Arts Councils and other state-supported museums and galleries are of immense value, it could be argued that these organisations in some way work to an agenda set by the Government that grants them their financial support. Artists who work with or for such organisations in turn have to meet certain criteria which are established and may be subject to change annually. Many artists are at odds with this structure, at odds with the notion of direct government involvement in their work and/or intentionally create work which doesn't fit the model. As a result these artists are often excluded from state patronage systems. Nevertheless such artists and their work, however complex, should not be overlooked.

Commissioning within Government, which normally means by the GAC, holds the potential to be challenging, perhaps ground-breaking, but is subject to even more political sensitivities than art commissioned through arms-length bodies such as the Arts Council or the Heritage Lottery Fund. Works that are overtly political, religious or have explicit content are problematic. Entropic works – works that are intended to deteriorate over time – temporary or ephemeral works such as performances, or works that attempt to affect the day-to-day running or processes of a department or building are at this point in time

fig.147
Martin Boyce
Paper Leaves and Concrete Trees,
2008
Burnished brass, and oxidised
acid-etched brass at the Ministry
of Justice (MoJ) headquarters in
Petty France, London

fig.148
Artist **Lothar Götz** installing
one of 51 unique wall paintings
titled *Round Trip* at MoJ

fig.149
Nathaniel Rackowe
LP13, 2008–09
Illuminated kinetic sculptural
installation at MoJ

fig.150
Conrad Shawcross
Axiom, 2009
Wooden sculpture with steel fixings
at MoJ

impossible to place. The immediate question would arise: what is public money being spent on and what will we have to show for it at the end? The answer is simple but not easily quantifiable: support of emerging British talent and the cultural economy, as well as a growing international reputation for leading the way in the visual arts. However there would be no lasting physical object as evidence. Fundamentally, it comes back to the age-old argument about the importance and value of the unique art-object.

A hundred and thirteen years on, government departments still prefer works of art that can be hung on walls, or stationed on a plinth in a central (but not too intrusive) location. Highly conceptual works or works that involve time-based media or audio-visual equipment are all but impossible for the GAC to commission. Not least because works that require projectors, monitors or electric motors are subject to the same stringent environmental controls as every other aspect of a public building and are usually reliant on management and maintenance by local staff. As a result such works are rarely commissioned and, when they are, they are often switched off to save on electricity costs. Nevertheless, there are many who fully understand the value of art in a building, including architect Michael Wilford:

> It is often the case that art is considered expendable, not as important as providing office space. However, working with artists in the way the GAC does to deliver commissions is a huge plus, a huge bonus… it's admirable. We end up with a better building than if we had not commissioned artists.[43]

At one time, artists were asked to deliver commissioned pieces with little more guidance than the dimensions their work should be. Today we expect even more of our artists, not only to assure us of the best quality and production values, but also to ensure their works are low cost and almost indestructible as well as offering an engaging visual experience and the all-important intellectual rigor. Artists should be able to produce something that is an 'exact fit' for a space which has yet to be built and is liable to change during the course of construction. The process is described by Marta Marcé, who was commissioned to create a new work for the British embassy in Madrid in 2009 (fig.151):

> The stairwell was still under construction while I was creating the work, so final details were not available until much later. This situation forced me to be very flexible and to develop and build on the relationships with the architects and the fabrication company that installed the final work. The results activated the stairwell and gave it a life of its own, enhanced the concept of constant movement and certainly provided a

fig.151
Marta Marcé
I am throwing the ball, 2009
Site-specific installation: self-
adhesive vinyl on glass panels
British embassy, Madrid

fig.152
A detail of **Catherine Bertola**'s
commissioned piece, *Frills
and Flounces*, 2006–07, at the
headquarters of the Department
for Culture, Media and Sport
(DCMS), London

fig.153
One section of **Simon Faithfull**'s
commissioned piece *Lea
Navigation*, 2006, at DCMS

fig.154
One section of **Henna Nadeem**'s commissioned piece *Heaven n Earth*, 2006–07, at DCMS

positive energy… and at the same time offered something playful for the viewer to engage with.[44]

On top of all this we expect documents, design drawings, engineering drawings and material specifications to be submitted by the artist in addition to the work of art, so that should the work be damaged, or in the worst case scenario destroyed, it would be possible to reconstruct it from scratch.

While the GAC commissions on the assumption that the work delivered will exist in perpetuity, the artist also has to accept that what was initially conceived as a site-specific project may not in fact end up being a site-specific artwork. In 2006 the Department for Culture, Media and Sport (DCMS) refurbished their offices in Cockspur Street, London. The GAC commissioned Catherine Bertola, Simon Faithfull and Henna Nadeem to create works that could be applied to the glass-walled offices (figs 152–154). In 2009 the DCMS vacated one floor of the building with the intention of letting that floor or possibly moving out

179

fig.155
Robert Holyhead's commissioned
piece *Untitled (Brussels)*, 2009,
showing the work in three different
configurations at the British
embassy, Brussels

altogether. Bertola, Faithfull and Nadeem's works may have to be removed, but the original designs and digital files will remain on the GAC's inventory so that when a new location becomes available, the GAC can discuss with the artist or their estate the practicalities of refabricating and re-siting the works.

These issues notwithstanding, commissioning by the GAC (or its predecessors) has given rise to some extraordinary projects and has provided numerous established and emerging artists with the possibility of working on a much larger scale than they had previously. To quote Marta Marcé again:

> It was a challenge, a very productive one, to produce a piece of work for a specific context, for a specific architecture, with specific aims, on a grand scale and working with a team instead of on my own in my studio. This is the kind of challenge where one learns to push boundaries, both conceptual and personal.[45]

Certainly the complexity of many contemporary spaces often presents artists with stimulating challenges. For example, the painter Robert Holyhead was asked to create a work for a glass wall and sliding door at the British embassy in Brussels in 2010. That he was approached for the commission in the first place came as a surprise:

> I was very curious about the idea of being commissioned as it had not occurred to me that this was something possible or indeed wanted within my practice. On the whole [I work] within the medium of oil paint and within the space of a canvas.[46]

Holyhead took into account the many possible positions of the door and created a work that delivered an elegant and coherent composition at all times regardless of the relative positions of the glass door to the glass wall (fig.155). For him, being approached by the GAC was an important factor in his considering the commission:

> The context for the commission was extremely important; the fact that it was the GAC and not a commercial conglomerate played a huge role in how I felt about it. I was being commissioned as an artist; the GAC's approach came from an understanding of my work and so the connection made sense.[47]

Over a century ago, MPs and government officials were very clear as to the benefits of unique works being produced specifically for presentation in government buildings in the UK and particularly abroad. By supporting artists, presenting them with challenges and providing opportunities for them to travel and create new works, the GAC continues this tradition. At the same time the GAC fosters experimentation and creativity and allows talent to flourish, offering a showcase for that talent around the globe.

NOTES

1. Deyan Sudjic, 'It's What's on the Inside that Counts', *Observer Review*, 16 July 2000.
2. In 1837 the Lord Chamberlain (Francis Conyngham, 2nd Marquess Conyngham) ordered a portrait of Queen Victoria to be painted by David Wilkie (1785–1841) who was at that time the Queen's Painter in Ordinary. The portrait was intended for the British embassy, Paris. It was not well liked by the Queen. Nevertheless it was displayed in Paris until 1847 when it was gifted to the then ambassador's wife (the Marchioness of Normanby and a former Lady of the Bedchamber to the Queen). Her Majesty's Office of Works and Public Buildings asked the artist William Corden to produce a copy of an 1843 state portrait of Queen Victoria, painted by Franz Xaver Winterhalter (ref. letter from Charles Noble, assistant to the Surveyor of the Queen's Pictures to Dr Mary Beal, curator, Government Art Collection, 23 April 1990, referring to Sir Oliver Miller's catalogue, *The Victorian Pictures in the Collection of Her Majesty the Queen*, Cambridge, 1992) – with the intention that it would replace the earlier portrait. Corden's copy was placed in the Paris embassy in 1847, later becoming part of the Government Art Collection, and has been on display there ever since.
3. Meirion and Susie Harries, *The War Artists* (London, 1983), p. 157.
4. Robert Russell Prentice (1883–1960) emigrated to Buenos Aires in 1910, returning to Britain at the outbreak of World War I. He returned to Argentina in 1919, establishing his own architect's practice. By 1925 he was appointed FRIBA and in the same year moved his practice to Rio de Janeiro.
5. The Adam style is an 18th-century neoclassical form of interior design and architecture, as practised by Scottish architects Robert and James Adam. The design of this building attracted some negative comments. Critics commented that the traditional style did not present Britain as a forward-thinking nation particularly as Brazil was creating ground-breaking architecture in its soon-to-be new capital of Brasilia.
6. Richard John Boileau Walker (1916–2010), art advisor to the Ministry of Works (1949–79) and curator of the Palace of Westminster (1950–76) followed in the footsteps of R. P. Bedford (retired keeper of the Department of Sculpture at the Victoria and Albert Museum), who was the first part-time curator appointed in 1947.
7. Letter from Foreign Office Chief Clerk Harold Caccia to Deputy Secretary of the Ministry of Works Sir Eric de Normann, 8 February 1949, GAC File AA 634/1 Part 2 / National Archive ref: WORK 54/58.
8. Piper had first been approached by the Ministry of Information and the War Artists Advisory Committee (WAAC) in 1940 when Leigh Ashton (former director of the Victoria and Albert Museum) asked Piper to produce a 'series of pictures of Air Raid Precaution control rooms'. The full extent of the involvement of the commissioners comes to little more than one line suggesting possible subject matter, notes that all sketches would have to be submitted for censorship, an indication that expenses would be covered and a fee of up to 100 guineas would be paid; David Fraser Jenkins, *John Piper: The Forties* (London, 2000), p. 29.
9. 'British Embassy at Rio De Janeiro: Decorations by John Piper', *The Times*, 6 October 1949, p. 7.
10. Internal note from Miss O. E. Cockett to Mr R. A. Barker, both of the Ministry of Works, requesting amendments to information drafted on the contents of the British Embassy, 9 June 1950, GAC File AA3058/1.
11. *A Special Exhibition of Five Paintings* by John Piper held at the Victoria and Albert Museum, London, 17 November 1949. The exhibition was open to the public from 18 November to 4 December.
12. *Evening News*, 29 November 1949.
13. Annual inventory check, GAC File AA3359/1.
14. Four of the Piper works were relocated to the residence of the British ambassador to the United Nations, New York, while one painting came back to London. In the early 1980s one work made its way back to Brazil, this time Brasilia, and by the late 1980s two of the other Piper works had returned to London while two others travelled to Oslo. In 2003 three works were installed at the ambassador's residence in Washington, DC, a fourth following in 2007. The fifth painting is currently displayed in the residence of the UK Representative to the European Union in Brussels.
15. Letter from David Eccles to Phillip Hendy (National Gallery), 24 July 1953, GAC File AA 631/1 Part 1.
16. Lowry had been commissioned by the WAAC in December 1942 and produced a painting titled *Going to Work for Mather & Platts*, an engineering company's Manchester factory. The WAAC also made a direct purchase of another Lowry work – a painting of the bombed-out St Augustine's Church, Manchester, June 1945. The former is in the collection of the Imperial War Museum, the latter held at Manchester City Art Gallery.

17. Letter from L. S. Lowry to David Carr, 8 June 1953, reproduced in Shelley Rohde, *A Private View of L. S. Lowry* (London 1979), pp. 232–233.

18. Ibid.

19. Letter from Pat Cooke (friend of Lowry) to Shelley Rohde, extracted in ibid., p. 233.

20. Ibid.

21. Letter from L. S. Lowry to Harold Macmillan, May 1955, from a copy of the letter in the Lowry Estate.

22. Letter from L. S. Lowry to Harold Wilson, 1967, from a copy of the letter in the Lowry Estate.

23. The PSA was an agency of the United Kingdom government, in existence from 1972 to 1993. Its role was to 'provide, manage, maintain, and furnish the property used by the government, including defence establishments, offices, courts, research laboratories, training centres and land', Property Services Agency, *Annual Report 1987–88*, HMSO.

24. As well as the PSA commissioning, the Pictures Section of the Department of the Environment – one of the previous incarnations of the GAC – continued to use its annual budget to acquire works of art.

25. Letter from R. Carr to E. S. Watson, 11 March 1976, GAC File SP 1687/13.

26. Originally set up as a small-scale venture in 1960 by two students at Cambridge, Paul Cornwall-Jones and Michael Deakin, Editions Alecto was at the centre of a movement promoting the idea that painters and sculptors should have the freedom to originate and realise their ideas in multiple form. Editions Alecto supported and promoted some of Britain's best known Pop artists.

27. Letter from Mrs M. Clarke to G. W. Harding, ambassador to Brazil, 8 April 1982, GAC File AA3359/1.

28. Dr Baron's suggestion anticipates the Arts Council of Great Britain's proposals for a Percent for Art Scheme in the UK by six years.

29. GAC File: BROADS Part 1, 14 November 1983.

30. Ibid.

31. Paolozzi treasured a recording of Britten's *Serenade for Tenor Horn and Strings*.

32. A text by Eduardo Paolozzi, 1986, GAC File BROADS/1 Part 1: commissions.

33. These works are discussed further by Richard Dorment in chapter 3.

34. Alex Hartley in a telephone conversation with Adrian George, GAC Curator, 1 December 2010.

35. Michael Wilford, architect, in an interview about the Berlin project with Nicky Hodge, GAC curator: Information & Research, 20 April 2010.

36. The PFI is a procurement method which provides private funding for public institutions in return for part-privatisation. Such projects aim to deliver infrastructure on behalf of the public sector, as well as associated services such as maintenance.

37. Letter from Alan Howarth, Minister for the Arts, to Baroness Scotland, Parliamentary Under-Secretary of State and Government Spokesperson for the Foreign and Commonwealth Office, 13 September 1999, GAC File $GEBEC Part 2.

38. Michael Binyon, 'Light on Moscow', *The Times*, 3 April 2000.

39. BBC Television News, 18 July 2000, broadcast at 10.33 GMT.

40. Rowan Moore, 'The House that Jack Built', *Evening Standard*, 28 November 2000.

41. A 'frit' is a ceramic composition that has been fused in a special oven, formed into a glass.

42. Basil Spence was a Scottish-born architect who had also designed the British embassy in Rome, the neighbour of 102 Petty France, Hyde Park Barracks, and – perhaps his best-known work – Coventry Cathedral.

43. Michael Wilford, architect, in an interview with Nicky Hodge, GAC Curator, Information and Research, 20 April 2010.

44. Marta Marcé in an email to the author, 17 September 2010.

45. Ibid.

46. Robert Holyhead in an email to the author, 21 September 2010.

47. Ibid.

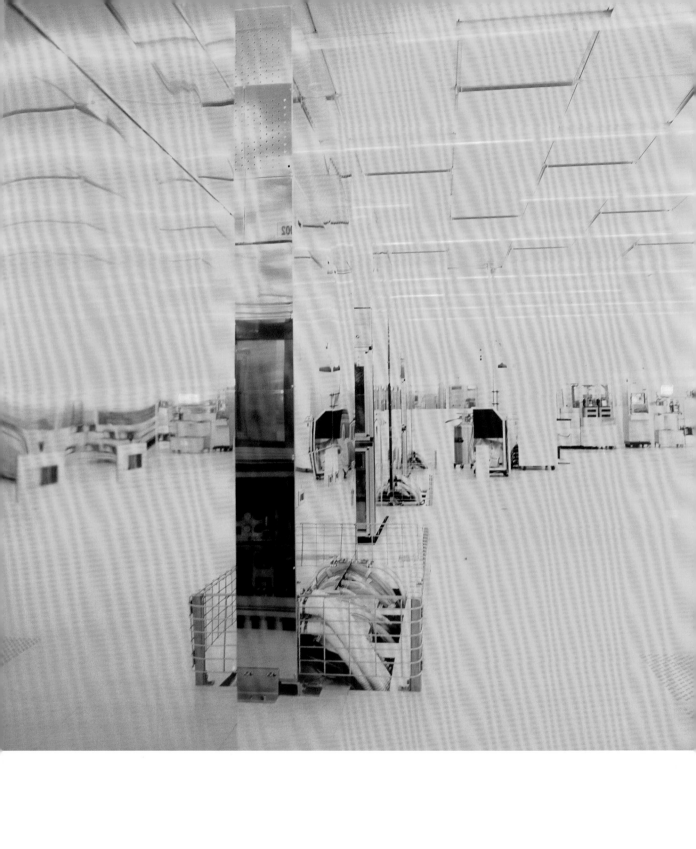

fig.156
Isaac Julien
*Fantôme Créole Series
(Papillon no. 1)*, 2005
Diptych of Lambda prints on
gloss paper

fig.157
Jane and Louise Wilson
Safe Light, Reflected Ballroom, 2003
C-type photographic print
on aluminium

fig.158
Catherine Yass
Embassy (day), 1999
Colour transparency and light-box

fig.159
David Tindle
Tea, 1970–1971
Acrylic on canvas

ACKNOWLEDGEMENTS

I would like to thank the following for their invaluable and much appreciated help in realising a long-held ambition to produce a book on the Government Art Collection (GAC):

Nicholas Serota for his foreword and Richard Dorment, Cornelia Parker and Andrew Renton for their insights into the Collection.

Ministers, Ambassadors and their staff, both past and present, for their contributions.

Our Ministers and colleagues in the Department for Culture, Media and Sport, in particular Ed Vaizey, Minister for Culture; Jonathan Stephens, Permanent Secretary; Andrew Ramsay, Director General, Partnerships; Mick Elliot, Director, Culture; Jane Cooper, former Director Publicity and Communications and Avril Holworthy, Communications Manager for their support.

Julia Somerville, Chairman, and members of the GAC Advisory Committee for their backing and encouragement.

Clive Lacey, Librarian, Foreign and Commonwealth Office for help with images.

All the artists and copyright holders who have given permission to reproduce their works of art.

Jenny McKinley, Oliver Craske and Sarah Kane at Scala Publishers Ltd.

Linda Lundin, Publication Designer at Park Studio.

GAC Team
Project Editor: Adrian George
Editor: Nicky Hodge
and Roger Golding, Robert Jones, Philippa Martin and Julia Toffolo
Images and additional photography: Tony Harris and Tung Tsin Lam

Penny Johnson
Director

CREDITS

INDEX OF ARTISTS